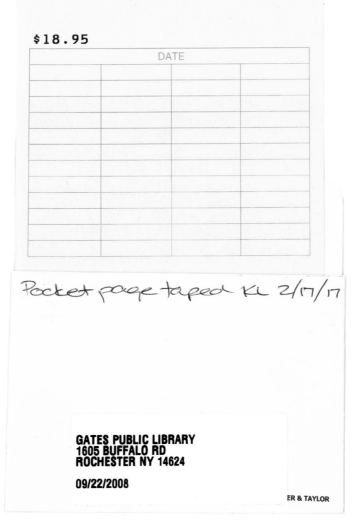

BALLS! Round 2

by

Michael J. Rosen

Illustrations by John Margeson

DARBY CREEK PUBLISHING

Text copyright © 2008 by Michael J. Rosen
Cover illustrations by John Margeson © 2008 by Darby Creek Publishing

Cataloging-in-Publication
Rosen, Michael J., 1954-
Balls! Round 2 / by Michael J. Rosen ; illustrations by John Margeson.
    p. ; cm.
ISBN 978-1-58196-066-2
Ages 10+.—Includes bibliographical references (p.) and index.—Summary: Learn about the balls used in baseball, softball, bowling, bocce ball, croquet, billiards, the shot put and other "oddballs": how they're made, why they look the way they do, some amazing facts about their history...and a bit about the games that use them, too.
1. Balls (Sporting goods)—Juvenile literature. 2. Ball games—Juvenile literature. [1. Balls (Sporting goods) 2. Ball games.] I. Title. II. Author. III. III.
GV749.B34 R674 2008
796.3—dc22
OCLC: 174958640

Published by DARBY CREEK Publishing
7858 Industrial Parkway
Plain City, OH 43064
www.darbycreekpublishing.com

Printed in Italy

2 4 6 8 10 9 7 5 3 1

BALLS! Round 2

From Sphere to There:
A Balls Round Up

In case you missed *Balls!*—which featured basketball, soccer, football, tennis, handball, golf, volleyball, and table tennis—*Balls! Round 2* just continues the investigation into those global wonders that put the "play" in playgrounds, the "grand" in grandstands, and the "tators" in spectators!

In this book, we'll trace the ancestors of eight more sports and/or game balls. We'll peek into each ball's fumbling failures, as well as the ball-designers' plans for their future. We'll dissect each ball, share some of the "ball talk" used in each game, discover how balls are molded or milled, and stop by the "BALL of Fame" to meet a few balls' most fanatical and famous handlers. I've also cooked up a few challenges that you can try at home, as well as some "Question-a-Ball" multiple-choice puzzles that explore some of the science that makes these balls spin. And, for good measure, I've tossed in a little BALLoney, just to keep you on your toes.

Forget ★ a ★ Ball

Not all balls are suitable for whacking with a mallet, catching in a glove, or rolling across the lawn—but does that make them spoiled sports? Not at all! There are hundreds of perfectly happy, non-sporting balls that you won't find here. But as a gesture of friendship, here's a salute to—gumballs, goofballs, mothballs, eyeballs, crystal balls, hairballs, meatballs, the balls of your feet, cotton balls, masquerade balls, melon balls, ballpoint pens, malted milk balls—you can go bonkers just thinking of all the balls under the sun! (Wait! The sun's another one!)

Catch Up

Now, just for fun, if you forced me to reduce the 72 pages of the original book, *Balls!*, into exactly 72 words—you would find out that . . .

- Squares stink at sports and don't bounce well.
- A basketball's 31,029 pebbles make it easier to grip.
- A taller person's ball bounces higher.
- Leaning forward will improve your chances at receiving a football.
- Handballs get warmer, softer, and bouncier throughout a game.
- In 18 holes of golf, the clubs touch the ball for 0.50 second—total.
- Volleyballs travel farther in summer and never whine about humidity.
- 168 table tennis balls weigh 1 pound.

And that's just a start. The other 19,238 words in *Balls!* tell the rest of the story.

DO Try This at Home! *The Science of Bounce-ability!*

All balls—sporting or not—have the potential to bounce. (Okay, meatballs don't bounce as high as, say, a tennis ball.) All they need is energy! And that begins with motion—falling or moving toward a surface. They just need to hold onto some of that energy when they get to the wall or floor in order to rebound. Sometimes balls lose energy as they squish and indent (think: meatball). The ball's molecules have to rush around in order to change the ball's shape and that steals energy and bouncing power.

The surface the ball is bouncing against also affects bouncing power. Soft surfaces—grass, snow, carpeting—cushion the ball, pad its landing, and absorb some of its energy. A concrete wall, wooden floor, or the basketball backboard don't absorb much energy, so the ball will use most of its incoming force to head right back out.

Here's a quick test so you can compare the bounces of as many balls as you can round up. Start with a variety—golf balls, Wiffle® balls, Superballs®, kitty toys—whatever you'd like. Next, you'll need an assistant; a measuring tape; a notebook for your results; and a wall that's next to a hard, flat surface, such as a tile or concrete floor, driveway, your brother's head (just kidding!).

Pin or tape the tape measure on the vertical surface, with the lowest number at the floor. (The plan is that you'll drop the ball near the tape measure, and your assistant will observe how high your ball bounces up and will write down the number in inches, or centimeters, if you prefer.) Ready?

1) Hold a ball from a set height. (For instance, hold the bottom of the ball at the 12" mark on the tape.)

2) Quickly release the ball. Don't give it any force, spin, or lift. Just let go.

3) Your assistant watches the ball bounce and looks at the highest point to record its "bounce."

4) Release each ball four times so you can find the average height of the ball's bounce-ability. (Just add up the results of your four bounces, divide by four, and you'll have your final result.)

5) Repeat with the other balls, one at a time, from the same starting height. Record all of the results.

What conclusions can you make about how "bounce-able" a ball might be? Can you also make predictions on: used vs. new balls, cold vs. warmed-up balls, hollow vs. solid balls . . . the list rolls on and on and on . . .

But it's time to have a ball with the rest of the book, so let's take a look.

What is "as American as apple pie" but actually comes from Australia, Portugal, France, and Costa Rica? LOOK!

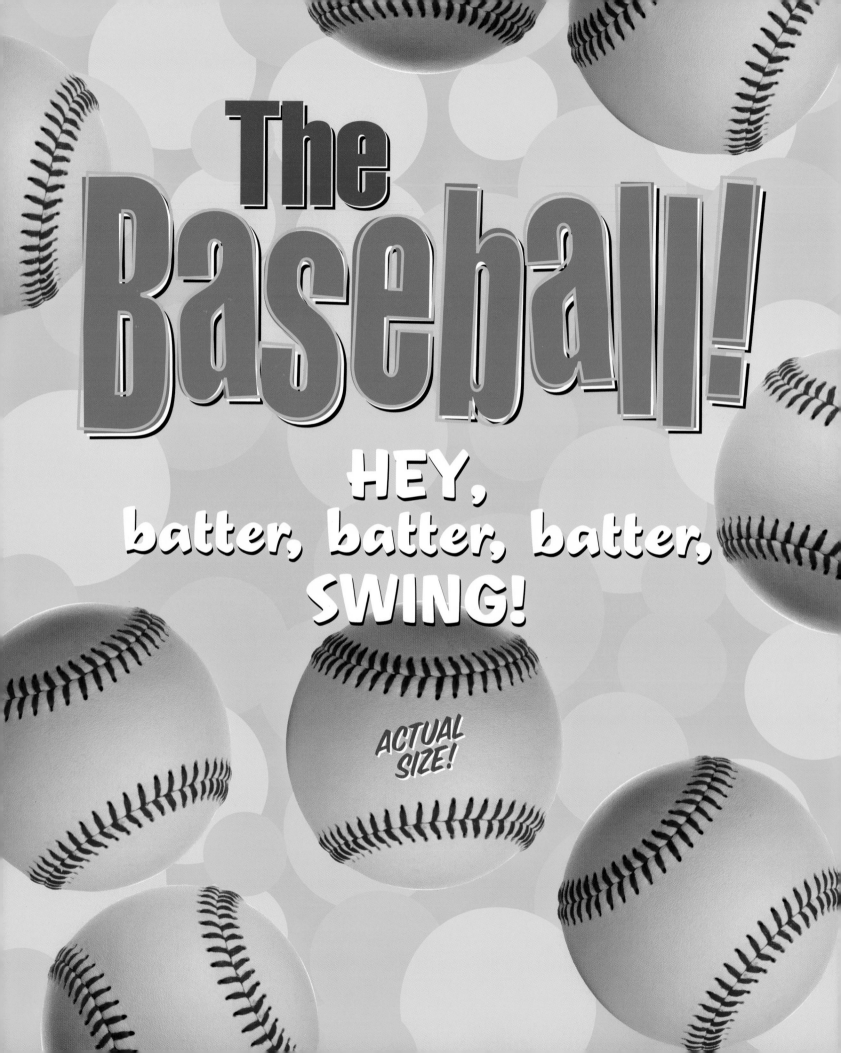

The Baseball!

HEY, batter, batter, batter, SWING!

ACTUAL SIZE!

Believe it or not, the millions of balls bought each season by American baseball teams—the Major League alone uses nearly 2 million balls—aren't made in America. The ball's inner cork is milled in Portugal, its rubber is tapped in Malaysia, its yarn windings are woven in Australia, its horsehide cover is tanned in France (cowhide covers do come from the States), and the ball is assembled in Costa Rica. So you could say that baseball has come a long way! Something close to 22,463 miles. On the other hand, 80 percent of the entire world's baseballs are produced in one place: China. They create the less-expensive balls used in little leagues and gym classes.

A vintage 1850–1860 "lemon-peel" style baseball.

Most baseball buffs agree that baseball arose from two games played in Great Britain: rounders and cricket. Rules of the American game, originally called "town ball," were unique to almost every ball diamond until the first rulebook was published in 1845.

The baseball we play and watch today is hardly the one played 150 years ago—or even 50 years ago, when a pitcher could sneak a ball into the freezer to harden the rubber center in hopes of defeating a great hitter's slam into the stands. Other oddities in baseball's wayward past include:

- Baseballs had a circumference of more than 10 inches. That's midway between today's hardball and softball.
- Defending teams could make an out by catching a ball on a fly or on the first bounce! And every hit ball was in play—fouls, too.
- Balls were pitched underhand. In 1884, when pitchers could throw overhand, batters wanted to even the odds and began to use flat-sided bats.
- Batters could ask pitchers to throw low or high (and they didn't even need to say, "Pretty-please with sugar on top?"). A player could swing at as many balls or wait out as many pitches—or even request a new pitcher—until his bat finally connected with a ball.
- The catcher stood 20 feet behind the batter. That might seem far away, until you remember that catchers wore no protective devices back then—not even a glove. (Not that anyone else wore gloves, either!)
- Hitting a bunt was considered unsportsmanlike and made the fans boo.
- Fielders used to drop balls on purpose to turn an easy out into a double play.
- A runner could be eliminated by soaking. No, not with a squirt gun or a hose. Just as in dodgeball, the fielding team could fire a ball at a runner who was not touching a base. Any guess why this play was also known as a "stinger"? Ouch!
- Pitchers cooked up every sort of "freak" delivery: spitball, shine ball, emery ball, and mud ball—anything that could change the ball's surface, and consequently, its speed and path.
- During baseball's first century, the number of foul pitches required to walk a batter were as many as 9. And the strike zone was wider: from the top of the shoulders to the bottom of the knees. (Today the ball has to come between the batter's armpit and the top of his knees.)

You'll never guess who gave the name "baseball" to the sport. (Go ahead, guess; we'll wait right here.) It was that great athlete of the pen, Jane Austen. In her 1916 novel Northanger Abbey, she referred to cricket and used the words "base ball."

That's the way the Ball Bounces

A Short History of the Baseball

What the Ball Was Called	When the Ball Was Used	What the Ball Was Made Of	How the Ball Responded	Other Cool Facts
The original handmade base-balls were known as **lemon-peel** balls and **belt balls**.	early and mid-1800s	String was wrapped around rubber strips and covered in horsehide. These balls were made by saddle- and shoemakers. The lemon-peel ball was made of four strips of leather sewn around a soft core. The belt ball was sewn from one H-shaped piece of leather.	Some balls were "dead" (they made a soft thud on the bat and rebounded sluggishly), while others really bounced, allowing some teams to score one hundred or more runs in a game.	The ball could weigh between 3 and 6 ounces and be as small as a plum or as large as a grapefruit.
Known as **dead balls**, the first standard balls marked an era of balls that tuck-ered out during a game.	1870s–1910	This rubber-core ball was wound in yarns and strings and then sewn into a horsehide cover. Balls wore out and softened during a game, so most teams hoped to score early when a batter had a better chance of sending a ball farther.	A ball absorbed so much of the bat's impact that low-scoring games were the norm, with many bunts, stolen bases, and hit-and-run plays.	In 1872, official ball size was established: They had to weigh between 5 and 5.5 ounces and have a circumference between 9 and 9.5 inches.
Long live the era of the liveliest ball yet, nick-named the **rabbit ball**!	1910–early 1920s	In 1910, a ball of cork was (secretly) introduced in the World Series and the advantage went to the hitters (a harder ball travels far-ther when hit). Also, during games, a ball took on so much dirt and moisture that it darkened and became hard to see.	This ball had go-power, bouncing off a bat with real energy and force. The number of batters who hit .300 tripled in one year. Babe Ruth hit 20 homers in 1919, 54 in 1920, and 59 in 1921.	After WWI, ball manu-facturers possessed better wool and more skilled workers. This combination made balls harder and able to travel farther.
In the era of the **"freak" ball**, pitchers cooked up **spitballs**, **scuffballs**, and **knuckleballs**.	mid-1920s–1930s	Because batters were sending balls far into the outfield, pitchers invented sneaky ways to deliver the ball and outwit the batter.	The number of balls in a typical game jumped from 3 or 4 to almost 60. The "freak" balls were outlawed in 1920.	Umps began inspecting balls, replacing scuffed balls, and rubbing balls with mud to reduce shine without scuffing.
Technology in the last seventy-five years contin-ues to tinker with the **modern ball**.	1930s–present day	To take some of the liveliness from the ball, raised stitches were added, which provided better grip and more rotation on the pitch. Around 1931, historians agree that the ball itself no longer favored either bat-ters or pitchers.	The ball underwent two more changes—for economic reasons. During WWII, there was a rubber shortage. For a short time, balls were made with a core of *balata*, a gum from Malaysia. This ball absorbed so much energy when hit—it dropped much sooner than a rubber ball—that ball teams refused to use them. One last change: In the 1970s, the covering switched from horsehide to cowhide.	A thin rubber wrapper was added around the core, also reducing the liveliness. Orange, yel-low, and red baseballs made a short appear-ance, but never caught on.
The **RIF ball** (Reduced Injury Factor), a safer ball, is used by young athletes.	mid-1980s	A core of polyurethane allowed balls to be made lighter. Also balls could be customized to meet the official weights of various leagues.	Balls weren't able to fly as far when hit, but they also didn't hurt as much if one accidentally hit a player!	These balls, adopted into the Little League in 1985, can still be pitched and hit well.

THE INSIDE SCOOP

The center "pill"
is a 0.5 ounce, grape-size cork. Thin layers of red and black rubber encase it, adding another 0.875 of an ounce.

Latex cement
holds the cover in place.

219 yards of yarn
windings create the ball's elastic and bouncy nature.
- 3-ply gray wool yarn
- 3-ply white wool yarn
- 4-ply gray wool yarn

Two white 8-shaped leather pieces
of cowhide or horsehide form the outer shell. (Synthetic fabrics cover less-expensive balls.)

150 yards of cotton-polyester yarn create a smooth outer layer to which the outer shell adheres.

The ball's weight
is 5 ounces; a leeway of 0.25 ounce is permitted.

108 rolled double stitches
of red, waxed, cotton thread bind the two parts of the shell. They are sewn by hand in about fifteen minutes. The first and last stitches are tucked back inside.

The circumference
is between 9 and 9.25 inches.

Bounce-ability
COR (a.k.a. coefficient of restitution) is a scale of elasticity—it is the measure of how far a ball will spring back when it strikes an immovable object. In fact, baseballs are fired from an air cannon at a speed of fifty-eight miles per hour (eighty-five feet per second) into a wall made of white ash, the wood used in most bats. The COR rating is the ball's initial speed (going toward the wall) compared to its rebound speed (coming off the wall). Major League balls have to rate 0.514 or 0.578, meaning they bounce back at a speed that's just over half as fast as they were shot. A higher rating means it's a harder ball with a higher bounce.

Squish-ability
Major League baseballs, when compressed with a force of 6.5 pounds, can't flatten more than 0.008 of an inch. (But when a hitter's bat delivers a blow to the ball, the force can be 8,000 pounds—and that compresses the ball in half!)

THE BiG UnWiND Up

A baseball's yarns are wound around the pill to create a diameter of 8.5 inches. It takes a machine to make such a precise ball out of more than 657 feet of squishy yarn! Too much tension pulls and thins the yarn. The result: a heavy ball because too much yarn was needed to make the regulation 8.5-inch diameter. Too little tension creates air within the loose windings. The result: a ball that's either too large (if it's the right weight) or too small (if it's the right size).

Most balls are wound with twisted wool. It's got two important powers: loft (it's fluffy) and memory (it's able spring back into shape). The most expensive

yarns are made with virgin wool, which is white and free of impurities. Gray wool contains other kinds of fibers, so it's a practical, cheaper alternative. Acrylic yarns (spun from petroleum, not sheep!) are even more economical, but they create balls that are even harder and livelier than wool-wound balls.

For Major League balls, wool must form eighty-five percent of the windings. First there are 121 yards of thicker, four-ply, twisted, blue-gray wool to build up the mass. Then there are 45 yards of thinner, three-ply, twisted, white wool. Finally, there are 53 more yards of a second color.

After all this dizzy winding, it's no wonder that a baseball likes to "unwind" a little on the ball field!

QUESTiON A BALL

Go for it!

Q: What on Earth—or in the earth!—is a GOPHER BALL? Is it ...

a.) a nickname for a very large marble?

b.) a fruit punch made with ginger ale and fruit juice?

c.) an easy pitch that the batter turns into a grand slam?

d.) a masquerade party where people dress up as their least-favorite animal?

A: Okay, since this is a book about balls, it would seem silly to talk about marbles, beverages, and costume parties, wouldn't it? So think of this as your warm-up question. The answer is **c**, an easy pitch that's destined to be a big hit!

The Seven Most Expensive Baseballs of All Time

(At Least for Now)

1. Mark McGwire's 70th home-run ball: $3,045,000

In 1998, St. Louis Cardinal slugger McGwire achieved the most home runs ever hit in a single season. A fan caught the ball. It was sold at an auction, where sports enthusiast Todd McFarlane (*shown here*, creator of the comic book/movie *Spawn*) was the highest bidder. The landmark ball sold for more than three million dollars.

2. Barry Bonds's 756th home-run ball: $752,467

In 2007, in front of 43,154 people, Bonds knocked pitcher Mike Bacsik's fastball into the centerfield bleachers, breaking the all-time homerun record set by Hank Aaron (*see below*).

3. Hank Aaron's 755th home-run ball: $655,000

Only five Major League hitters can claim more than 600 career homers. (Willie Mayes hit 660, Babe Ruth hit 714, Hank Aaron hit 755, and Barry Bonds [*above*] and Sammy Sosa [already past 600] are still slugging away.) Aaron's record held from 1974 to 2007.

4. Sammy Sosa's 66th home-run ball: $150,000

At that time—1998—no one had hit more home runs than Chicago Cubs player Sammy Sosa. The buyer? Once again, it was Todd McFarlane. (He owns 5 of the 10 most expensive baseballs.)

5. The first home-run ball ever hit at Yankee Stadium: $126,500

The ball was hit in 1923 by none other than Babe Ruth himself. It just took 75 years for the ball to be sold.

6. Mickey Mantle's first home-run ball: $117,899

On May 1, 1951, the 21-year-old Yankees rookie, Mickey Mantle, scored his first homer. The catcher handed him the scoring ball. Mantle kept it, and inscribed it: "My first H.R. in the Majors, May 1, 1951, 4:50 p.m. Chicago" and "6th inning off [pitcher] Randy Gumpert."

7. The ball that a fan knocked out of Moisés Alou's glove: $106,600.

In 2003, during Game 6 of the National League Championship Series, Moisés Alou runs to catch a fly ball, glides up the wall with his glove extended high—but a bunch of Cubs fans, including one Steve Bartman, are also reaching for the ball. Bartman bumps Alou's glove, knocking the ball into the stands. What might have been an out becomes a home run. The Cubs, who had been headed to the World Series for the first time since 1945, lose that game (as well as Game 7), giving the Marlins a chance in the World Series.

Fossum Flips, Folly Floaters, Hesitation Hummers, Slurves, Forkballs, Eephus Balls, and Other More Common Pitches

Every pitcher adds a personal touch to each throw. Like fingerprints, no two pitched balls are ever the same, even if they're both, say, fastballs. Pitchers who perfect a certain throw often give it a new name, such as the ones mentioned in the title above. Yes, they're all Major League pitches that travel between 50 and 130 miles per hour.*

So how is the same ball served up at the plate in so many different ways? In addition to the speed, the moment of release, and follow-through, the pitcher's finger position, wrist tension, and grip placement in relation to the ball's stitches create shifts in a ball's path.

Now, batter up! Let's look at the basic pitches that might come across the plate.

Main photo: Fastball grip, inset: curveball grip

1. fastball: A fastball spins 1,600 times in a minute, although a typical pitch only completes about eleven rotations in the half second that it takes to fly from the pitcher's mound to home plate. Pitchers must aim slightly upward to throw this "straight-line ball" because, even as the ball moves eighty-five to ninety-five miles per hour, gravity pulls it downward 2.5 feet in that half-second journey.

2. curveball: A curveball spins 1,800 or more times in a minute, usually making fifteen turns before it crosses the plate. A pitcher's middle finger pushes on the outer seam, and the fingers "snap" as the wrist twists downward as the ball is released. This creates a topspin that causes the ball to drop. The more spin, the more curve. A great curveball can veer seventeen inches before it reaches the plate, and most of the curving happens right before the batter swings!

*You think that sounds fast? Just for comparison, if you're a typical ball-playing kid in the neighborhood, your pitch travels thirty or forty miles per hour. But check this out: Your bat—when it connects with the ball—typically vibrates back and forth 170 times in a single second.

3. slider: A slider spins 1,700 times per minute (thirteen of them on the way to the plate), whirling from left to right at about eighty-five miles per hour. The pitcher releases a slider with sidespin—think of how a quarterback sends a football into the air—so that it swerves five or ten inches toward third base as it approaches the batter.

4. knuckleball: A knuckleball spins only twenty-five to fifty times in a minute—not even one complete rotation on the way to the plate. This allows the air flowing around the ball to shift abruptly, jogging this way or that—often two or more times—before it crosses the plate. The pitcher grips the ball with his fingertips (not the knuckles!) and releases the ball at only sixty-five miles per hour.

5. screwball: Delivering a screwball, the pitcher twists his wrist inward—that's opposite to the way a curveball is thrown. This unnatural movement strains the arm, but it allows a right-handed pitcher to deliver a screwball that suddenly breaks away from a left-handed batter.

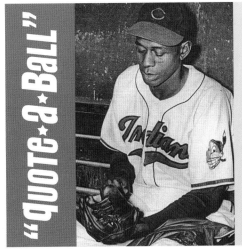

"QUOTE·A·BALL"

"My pitching philosophy is simple—keep the ball away from the bat."

—legendary pitcher Satchel Paige, perhaps the most entertaining storyteller in baseball's history

BALL of FAME

Perfect Pitch(er)

Who: John Lee Richmond, originally from Ohio, playing for the Worcester, Massachusetts Ruby Legs

Record: In 1880, Richmond threw the first perfect game in American baseball, defeating the Cleveland team. ("Perfect" means no hits, no players on bases, and no runs by the opposing team.)

Who else: John Montgomery Ward, another pitcher, threw the second perfect game in baseball history 5 days later. That's eighteen innings in which the balls escaped with nothing more than a few little foul-ball bumps.

Far Flung

Who: Canadian Glen Gorbous

Record: On August 1, 1957, Glen delivered the longest throw in baseball history—a flight of 445 feet, 10 inches.

Who else: Mildred "Babe" Didrikson made the women's longest throw. On July 25, 1931, she fired a baseball 296 feet.

Speed Demon

Who: (Lynn) Nolan Ryan of the California Angels

Record: He pitched the first ball that broke a speed of 100 miles per hour. On August 20, 1974, his ball flew across the plate at 100.9 miles per hour. Since that time, nearly three dozen pitchers have fired faster balls; the fastest has reached 104 miles per hour.

What else: With the longest career in baseball history—from 1966 to 1993 on four different teams, including the Texas Rangers—Ryan holds the unofficial title of "Strike-out King." Ryan's pitches caused 5,714 players to whiff out at the plate.

"quote-a-ball"

"Every strike brings me closer to the next home run."

—*George Herman "Babe" Ruth, one of the U.S.'s most celebrated athletes and baseball's first great slugger*

BALL TALK

The Pitches

backdoor slider: *a ball that seems well out of the strike zone, but suddenly breaks back across the plate (and is too late to swing at!).*

cheese, heat, heater: *nicknames for a fastball.*

yakker, Uncle Charlie: *nicknames for a curve ball.*

chin music: *a ball that crosses the plate high and inside.*

meatball: *a ball that floats right across the plate and is easy to hit.*

pea: *a ball batted or thrown at very high speed.*

The Hits

can of corn*: *a ball that a fielder can nab very easily.*

rope or frozen rope: *a hard line drive the batter sends across the infield.*

seeing-eye single: *a soft ground ball that slips between the infielders, putting the batter on first.*

Texas leaguer: *a nice hit that lands just as the out-fielder and the infielder yell, "I thought YOU had it!"*

blast, dinger, dong, four-bagger, four-base knock, moon shot, tape-measure blast, and tater: *nicknames for that sweetest word in baseball—a home run.*

* Why would a can of corn mean an easy catch? Back when customers waited at the counter while the grocer filled their shopping list, to get a can stacked on a high shelf, a clerk would jab it with a broom handle and catch it in his apron.

DO Try This at Home!

DouBALL TrouBALL!

One of the greatest sluggers of all time, the Yankees' Babe Ruth, began his career as a pitcher. Ever the show-off, he could throw two baseballs at once. The balls would travel at the same speed, parallel to one another, and land at the same instant in the catcher's glove. (Of course, he never threw this particular pitch in a league game.)

Next time you're playing catch, give it a try—but only throw the two balls against a fence or where no one is standing. That is, until you can throw as well as the Babe.

QUESTION A BALL

Are You Even in the Ballpark?

Q: On average, how many baseballs does a Major League baseball team purchase each year?

a.) about 200

b.) about 3,000

c.) about 18,000

d.) depends on how many sluggers in their club routinely knock balls out of the stadium

A: The answer is **c**, about 18,000, although some clubs claim to use more than 40,000. Typically seventy-two balls are readied for each game.

Let's Keep It Clean!

Q: According to the Major League's Official Rules, which "foreign substances" are pitchers forbidden from applying to a ball?

a.) rosin (a sticky solid made pine sap)

b.) soil (dirt)

c.) paraffin (the waxy stuff of candles)

d.) licorice (the black candy lots of people don't like, but I do!)

e.) emery paper (the sandpaper on fingernail files)

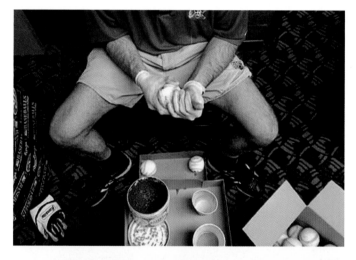

A: The answer? They're all listed. If the umpire finds a ball that's been deliberately discolored or tampered with, he removes the offender from the game immediately. And if a pitcher throws such a manipulated ball to a batter, the umpire suspends him for ten days. There is one substance that is approved: Lena Blackburne Baseball Rubbing Mud, a goop that comes from a tributary of the Delaware River and looks like gritty chocolate pudding. This same mud is rubbed on and has reduced the gloss on all Major League balls since the 1950s. These days, each team spends about one hundred dollars for six pounds of the stuff per season.

Your Hard Life as a Major League Baseball

Day One: The home team crew unwraps your tissue paper package like a diaper on a newborn baby: Welcome to the stadium, brand-new ball! Someone rubs your bald surface with mud to reduce your shine and slickness. You're ready to meet the world.

Day Two: It's your big day. The pitcher tucks you into his pocket. He cups you in his hands, slams you a couple times into his mitt, and positions his fingers to deliver the pitch. In an instant, you're flying across the plate and . . .

You're a hit . . . slammed over the infield . . . the outfield . . . and into the cupped hands of an eager fan, never to be seen again . . . **OR**

You're a ground ball, bounced across the turf, scooped up by the short stop, tossed over to first! Then you're tossed to the second baseman, who tags out a runner, and tosses you over to the catcher. Whew! You're a little scuffed up. Time to sit out. **OR** . . .

You're a bunt, a foul, or just a perfect strike caught in the catcher's mitt. In any case, you're in line for a few more tosses.

And at the end of the day, your Major League career is over. Thanks so much, see you 'round.

Day Three: Retirement's not so bad: You get to join batting practice. A couple of batters will give you their best shots. And then, that's enough of that.

(If you're an especially lucky ball—just a few grass stains and marks—you get a quick scrubbing up in a tumbling drum filled with chunky erasers. Cleaned up, you earn another day of practice.)

Days Four, Five, and Six: Welcome to the indoor batting cages! Life's a bit tougher now. Over the new few days, you're going to be slammed around quite a lot. Try not to lose your cool.

Day Seven: You're off to the farm—a farm team, that is. Packed into a bag with your colleagues, you'll have a whole new life with a Minor League team where you'll be pitched, batted, tossed around the field, and slammed into gloves. Then, one day, your stitches splitting, your skin scarred and dark, it's off to that big ballpark in the sky. It's a tough life, full of hard knocks, but you were born to do it!

What ball has answered to the names "mush," "pumpkin," "lightning," "Army," "diamond," and, most popularly, "kitten"?

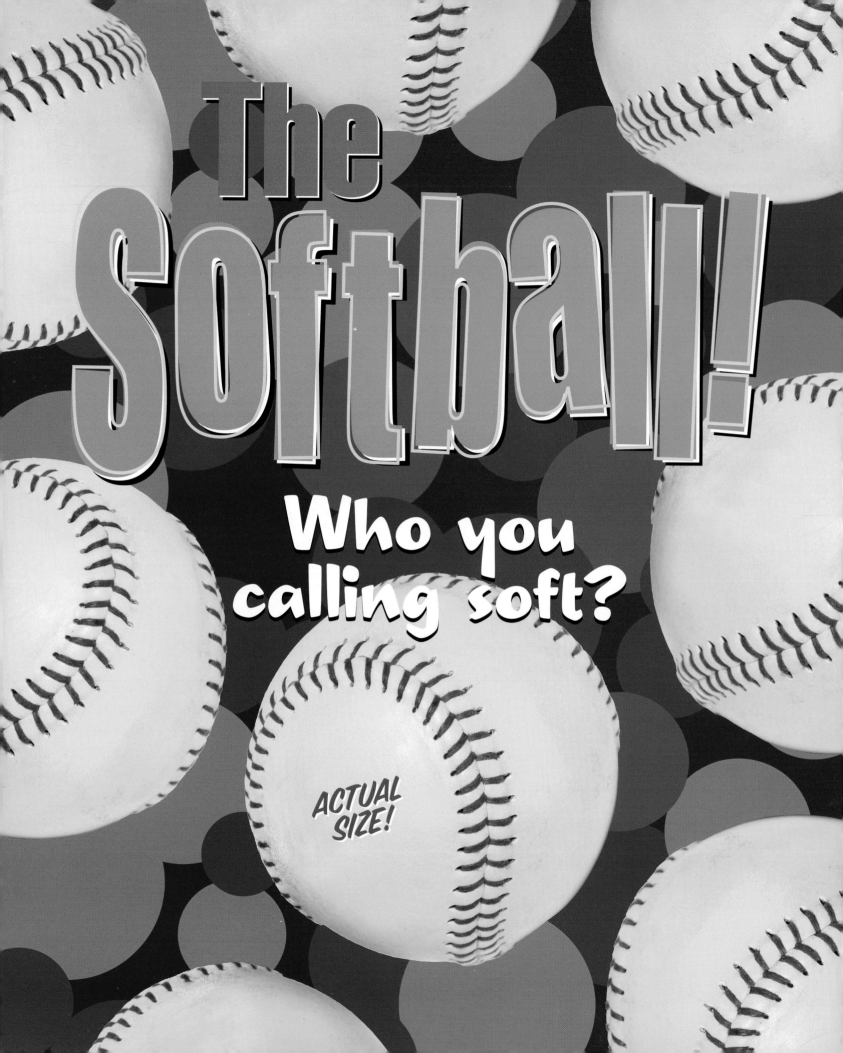

The Softball!

Who you calling soft?

ACTUAL SIZE!

You might not guess that the number-one team sport in this country, played by more than forty million people every season, is softball. Or that it all began one afternoon, almost by accident, and took on a life independent of its big brother, the more expensive game of baseball. Indeed, the very success of softball is that it can be played or watched without much expense: no uniforms, no huge stadiums and pricey tickets, and no limit to the number of teams, leagues, or titles that can join in the new game. Athletes of all ages and abilities can usually find a nearby softball team.

If you watch how the ball itself has evolved over 120 years, you get a good picture of this sport's history. So let's turn the tale over to old softie himself.

In the Beginning...

The first softball was a boxing glove "stitched" with its laces into a sphere that was played by football fans at a boating club. As the story goes, a Yale grad tossed a boxing glove toward the Harvard men, and one of them, George Hancock, grabbed a broom handle and swatted it back. Thus, on Thanksgiving Day 1887, on a chalk-marked field inside the Farragut Boat Club in Chicago, the first softball game was held.

Hancock's game continued to be played, indoors and then outdoors, with new rules that allowed the game to adapt to a larger ball and a smaller playing field. Called a *clincher*, the first true softball was about sixteen inches around, although various teams used balls ranging in size from ten to twenty inches around.

In nearby Minneapolis, a fire department league used a small medicine ball and created another version of the game. They called it "Kitten League Ball," after the organizer's team, the Kittens. But by 1926, the name "softball" was winning out over the other names—"diamond ball," "indoor-outdoor," or "kitten ball." Alongside the 1933 World's Fair, fifty-five teams from across the country came to Chicago for a tournament in men's and women's slow-pitch, and men's fast-pitch. They used a ball with a fourteen-inch circumference and established a new organization, the Amateur Softball Association. The ASA formally agreed that the game, from then on, should be called "softball"—and enough already with the kitten jokes!

How to Make a Softball in Five Easy Steps

1 Begin with a traditional cork core or with the newer and larger solid polyurethane core. With cork cores, an additional layer of twisted yarn is wound around it just as with baseballs. Polyurethane cores don't require yarn windings.

2 A string cover is wrapped by machine around the entire ball; it's then secured in place with a coating of latex or rubber cement.

3 Two 8-shaped leather covers for each ball are punched out of tanned hides and perforated with small holes where the stitching thread will run. These covers are paired up.

4 The ball and its covers are held in place with clamps and temporary staples. Often the leather is moistened so when dried, it will shrink to a taut sphere. Two needles stitch the covers together tightly.

5 Finished balls are inspected, stamped with league's seal and the manufacturer's name, boxed up, and shipped off.

GOLDILOCKS AND THE THREE SOFTBALLS???

This One Is Too Soft

The core of early softballs was formed with long strands of kapok, a cottony tree fiber. This core was covered in yards of yarn windings and then sealed inside a stitched leather cover. Unfortunately, these "mush balls," as they were called, didn't travel very far. Even though the game's original idea was to have a ball that allowed easier catches of slower balls (as compared with baseball), players still wanted a livelier ball.

This One Is Too Hard

In 1975, the softball's firmness was vastly improved when its core was switched from compacted kapok fluff to cork and polyurethane. Yarn was still wrapped around the ball before the leather cover was glued and sewn in place. But soon enough, softball became a game of homers! Even slower swingers were consistently knocking these balls over the fence—and often shattering their bats in the process. (And those high-tech bats cost $300 or more.)

This One Is Just Right

High-compression balls to the rescue! In 2003, creating a major and much-needed change, these balls were harder than a baseball—and harder to knock out of the sandlot. But even the strongest batters were frustrated by this ball. More fine-tuning was still needed. Within two years, the Dudley sporting goods company rolled out the Thunder Advance, which added a layer of urethane foam between the cover and the core. This cushion absorbed some of the bat-ball vibration, deadening this 21st-century ball just enough so that games were neither all homers with very little fielding or low-scoring innings with all infield outs.

And so, today's balls, as well as today's bats, can last more than a single inning of play!

"QUOTE-A-BALL"

"The only real difference between baseball and softball is that when you get hit by a softball, it leaves a bigger mark."

—Anonymous

THE INSIDE SCOOP

The leather cover
(white or "optic yellow") of cowhide or horsehide is formed from two 8-shaped pieces. They are pebble-textured, perforated along the edges, and stitched together. (Synthetic covers are also permitted.)

A 0.125-inch-thick mantle
made of urethane foam under the cover absorbs a bit of the power.

The weight
of a 12-inch ball is between 6.25 and 7 ounces; for an 11-inch ball, it's 6 ounces, with a 0.125-ounce allowance.

A hard inner core
of polyurethane gives the ball its traveling power. (Other balls have cork-and-yarn cores or kapok fibers.)

The circumference
of the ball is 12 inches around or 11 inches for youth leagues with a 0.125-inch leeway.

Eighty-eight stitches
close up the cover.

Bounce-ability: Softballs must have a specific elasticity. When fired from an air cannon at 60 miles per hour, the softball must have a rebound speed that's either 40 or 47 percent of its initial speed—that's a rating of 0.40 or 0.47.

Squish-ability: Softballs are rated for firmness. In a squeeze test, weight is applied to a rod that presses into a ball until it reaches a depth of 0.25 inch. Harder balls, which travel farther, require more weight to dent. Pro softballs require a rating between 375 and 400 pounds.

grudge Match!

It's Hardball vs. Softball

The game of softball differs from the game of baseball in some big and not-so-big ways. But from the ball's point of view, the main differences are that in softball...

- ...fewer balls are used in a shorter game.
- ...fewer balls are hit into the stands.
- ...the game is played on a smaller diamond with a smaller bat.

- ...a shorter throwing distance exists between bases (30 feet instead of 60 feet).
- ...a pitcher throws pitches underhand from a spot that's 13.5 to 19.5 feet closer.

How do the balls measure up in our grudge match? Check out these facts:

TYPE OF BALL	Baseball	Fast-pitch softball	Slow-pitch softball
STITCHES	108 raised-seam red stitches	88 flat-seam white stitches	88 flat-seam white or red stitches
THREAD	104 inches of waxed cotton, doubled	104 inches of waxed cotton or linen, doubled	104 inches of waxed cotton or linen, doubled
CIRCUMFERENCE	9 to 9.25 inches	11.875 to 12.25* inches	11.875 to 12.25* inches
WEIGHT	5 to 5.25 ounces	6.25 to 7 ounces	6.25 to 7 ounces
PITCH DELIVERY	Any method is allowed: overhand, underhand (also called "submarine"), and sidearm (throwing at a height between the shoulder and hip, parallel to the ground). It's rare for Major League pitchers to throw all three.	Pitchers rule this game. They throw fastballs underhand, usually with a "windmill" or "slingshot" delivery. (Modified Pitch Softball allows fast pitches, but, as in slow-pitch, a pitcher's feet remain together, hips facing the batter, with no windmill wind-up.)	Batters get the edge in this game. Pitches are all underhand with no "windmill" wind-up permitted. Pitcher's feet remain together, hips facing the batter. To keep pitches from being too fast, balls must also arc upwards between 6 and 12 feet on the way to the plate.

*Slow-pitch leagues use a "cushier" 16-inch white ball, weighing between 9 and 10 ounces. A smaller, lighter ball is in play in many youth leagues: Balls must be 11 inches around (with 0.25 inch allowance) and weigh 6 ounces (with 0.25 ounce allowance).

Go for it!

Q: How far can you fly, ball?

Bases are loaded. You, the team's power hitter, are at the plate. Everyone's counting on you to knock a ball out of the stadium. Do you have a better chance if you're playing in Denver, Phoenix, Atlanta, or New Orleans? In other words, can your teammates count on you to slug the ball...

a.) the same distance no matter where you are playing?

b.) farther in the two western ballparks (Phoenix and Denver)?

c.) farther in the two eastern ballparks (Atlanta and New Orleans)?

d.) and just run to first base and quit thinking about questions like this?

A: If you really want to be a power hitter who can blast a softball out of the stadium—that's 200 yards—play in a vacuum-sealed ballpark. What slows down a ball and forces it to drop more quickly to the ground is air and wind.

Without the air's drag and resistance, you could send a ball sailing beyond the outfield fence—and well beyond that!

But since you'd only have about ten seconds to play softball in a vacuum before your body called time out for good (trust me, you don't want to know the gory details), we'd better consider your options at these four other ballparks.

Even though there's air and wind over all four fields, each city is located at a different altitude. The higher the playing field, the thinner the air. Thinner air means less drag, which means your ball can travel farther. In fact, for every 1,000 feet you are above sea level, your ball will travel about seven feet farther. Playing in Denver, which is 5,280 feet above sea level, your ball gets the biggest boost from the thinnest air: It will travel about nine percent farther than it will in New Orleans. Phoenix is located at next highest altitude (1,100 feet above sea level). Atlanta is 1,000 feet above sea level. And New Orleans, just about *at* sea level, is the home of your shortest hit. So you have your best chances of a homer where the air is thinner—at the two ball parks out west. Thus, the correct answer is **b**.

Keep Your Eye on the Ball!

You're standing at the plate. The pitcher is winding up. The coach yells, "Keep your eye on the ball!" Okay—but *can* you? I mean, really?

Well, sports fans, the answer is no, even if your typical Little League pitcher's ball only travels 40 miles per hour, instead of a pro's 90 or even 100 miles per hour. It simply takes more time for a batter to complete a swing than for a ball that has left the pitcher's hand to arrive—*fwap!*—in the catcher's mitt.

Your incredibly fast eyes aren't fast enough to track a ball that can sail past with an angular velocity (that's the speed that something moves across your field of vision) of more than 500 degrees in a second. Most eyes can only track an object for 70 degrees in a second. (Some great batters have trained themselves to see 120 degrees in a second, which does let them keep their eye on the ball a bit longer.)

So, you're standing at the plate. In the half second between the pitch and your swing, you will probably take:

- 0.1 second to evaluate how the ball is leaving the pitcher's hand.
- 0.1 second to decide if and how you're going to swing.
- 0.25 to 0.40 second to complete your swing.

Basically, that's 0.2 seconds to "keep your eye on the ball." After that, you can close your eyes if you'd like, because your muscles won't receive any more information on how to position and swing the bat.

Try this experiment:

You need an indoor ball (such as a Nerf® ball), a bat, two friends, and a ball-friendly indoor place that can be darkened.

1. Have a friend pitch you a few easy balls and practice a little batting. Then keep track of how many times you hit the same easy ball in 10 pitches.

2. Ask your *other* friend to stand at the light switch. You're now going to try 10 more easy pitches, but this time, at the exact moment your friend sees the ball leave the pitcher's hand, he turns out the lights. He's got to be quick! Meanwhile, you continue your swing. Lights on, find the ball, get back in position, get ready for the next pitch…then lights off again, and swing!

Did you hit approximately the same number of balls, lights on or off? Switch positions and see if your friends have the same experience.

BALLS of FAME

Switch Pitcher

Who: Ben Crain of Des Moines, Iowa

Record: An incredible athlete, Ben pitched softballs either right-handed or left-handed in almost 1,000 games—100 of them no-hitters—during a career that lasted from 1928 to 1951. He even pitched double-headers—he'd use his right arm for one game and his left arm for the next.

What's so great: You've heard of switch hitters—batters who can swing right-handed from one side of the plate or left-handed from the other side—but switch pitchers are rare. In baseball, you can count professional ambidextrous pitchers on one hand: Tony Mullane (who played without a glove, holding the ball with both hands, and firing it toward the plate either right- or left-handed), Larry Corcoran, and Elton "Icebox" Chamberlain. The one 20th-century pitcher, Greg Harris, only got to pitch with both arms for a single inning in 1995.

Softball's Six-Foot-Tall Sensation

Who: Jennie Finch of Arizona

Record: Considered by many to be the best softball pitcher in the world, Jennie is a two-time Olympic gold medalist and holds the NCAA record for winning 60 games in a row.

What else: Jennie's signature pitch is her riseball—basically, an upside-down curve ball that has enough backspin to rise as it reaches the plate. Fired at 70 miles per hour, Jennie's ball has even struck out Major League baseball players.

In what game can your ball bring you a turkey? Or better yet, a wild turkey? Or best of all, a golden turkey?  LOOK!

The Bowling Ball!

Three strikes*... and you're in!

ACTUAL SIZE!

*in bowling lingo, three strikes is "a turkey," six strikes is "a wild turkey," and nine strikes is "a golden turkey."

Rolling one thing at a bunch of other things must be as natural to human beings as tapping a foot to a great beat or scratching a bug bite. It's easy to imagine the first upright creatures rolling a rock toward a row of pinecones or lobbing an orange at a line of pointy seashells.

In the 1930s, anthropologist Sir Flinders Petrie discovered a ball and pins in a mummified child's grave dating from 3200 BC. He concluded that Egyptian children rolled those crude balls at the crude pins and were counting on there being bowling alleys in the afterlife.

Artifacts also revealed that a bowling game was enjoyed in Germany around 300 AD. (This was even before there were proper bowling shoes and swell bowling shirts—hard to imagine, but true.) There are also documents showing that England's King Edward III forbade the game in 1366 because, for whatever reason, his troops preferred to roll balls at pins than to practice firing arrows at their armed enemies.

When European settlers brought bowling to America, their game needed only nine pins—which is why they called it "ninepins." By 1841, the sport had become such a popular form of gambling that Connecticut outlawed "ninepin lanes," hoping to end the gambling. Rather than give up their sport, bowlers had another idea: "If we just add one more pin, we won't be playing ninepins!"

Tenpin bowling caught on, although it took another five decades until, in 1895, the American Bowling Congress gathered bowling-club representatives from around the country to agree on standards for ball weight, pin size, game rules, and the exact number of ounces for an extra-large soft drink at the lane's snack bar.

Bowling was on a roll! In 1951, pinspotter machines replaced pinboys—kids who worked behind the alleys to set up and remove fallen pins for each frame. "Make that Spare" and other bowling programs filled the channels of that new exciting invention, the television! Bowling grew so popular that some stock-market investors in 1961 predicted that every person in the United States would soon be bowling two hours every day. (So, they were wrong.) Today, bowling alleys struggle to draw in as many bowlers as they once did, even though the sport boasts more than ninety-five million regular participants in more than ninety countries.

Maybe you're still thinking that bowling doesn't require real athletic ability. Consider this: During a three-day pro tournament, bowlers roll a fifteen-pound ball a distance of sixty feet and must hit the pins' target zone within half an inch. And they must do this nearly nine hundred times. That's a total weight of more than six tons! (And missing that target fewer than one hundred times in order to be a real contender.) Bowlers need muscle strength, mental concentration, coordination, and years of training.

And there are new bowling innovations all the time. Like Cosmic Bowling. A mysterious smoke suddenly fills the bowling alleys. (Cue the fog machine.) The building rumbles, pounds, and clashes. (Cue the dance music; lower the giant speakers.) Stars and rainbows skid across the walls and ceiling. (Cue the laser light show.) Your bowling ball glows pink, the lane shimmers purple, and the pins gleam eerily like skull's teeth. (Cue the strobes and black lights.) Yes, bowling becomes an entirely novel experience when the balls, pins, and lanes are treated with an ultraviolet coating—all to make you feel as if you're bowling among the stars. At least until Dad pulls up in the car to bring you back to Earth.

The "Change-a-Ball"

The earliest bowling balls were stones—nothing more than the roundest rocks lying around. Probably the first bowlers, like Fred Flintstone and Barney Rubble at the Bedrock Bowl-O-Rama, figured out that a less-bumpy sphere rolled straighter, so they learned to chip and sand the ball into a smoother sphere.

The next bowling balls were carved from a tropical evergreen tree, *Lignum vitae* (that's Latin for "long life"). Sometimes called ironwood, this is the planet's hardest wood, which is also made into many other sporting balls, house posts, ribs for sailing ships, butcher blocks, and gavels.

Early in the 1900s, the first rubber bowling ball, Evertrue, was molded rather than carved. The rubber added springiness to the roll. In 1914, scientists at Brunswick created "a mysterious rubber compound" especially for bowling balls, and the Mineralite ball bounced onto lanes everywhere. For the first time, a bowler could count on a ball's speed and precision. By 1960, bowling alleys stocked hard rubber balls in colors (usually red, blue, and black), and in weights ranging from six to sixteen pounds.

The biggest change arrived in the 1970s with polyester. Not only could a bowler wear a vibrant polyester leisure suit to the lanes, but he could also throw a polyester ball that allowed a very straight approach to the pins with almost no hook at the end. (Lanes are frequently oiled, particularly the first two-thirds of their length. Since polyester balls weren't affected very much by the slippery surface, bowlers often chose this ball when they wanted a straight shot for making a spare or for when a lane seemed dry and other balls were hooking too much.)

Balls with a urethane coverstock appeared a decade later. These durable, but expensive, balls were easy to maintain, predictable to throw, and custom-drilled to meet each bowler's needs in terms of skid, hook, and action. Until that point, most bowling balls were formed in three pieces: a pancake-like core, a less-dense core material poured around that, and then a surrounding outer coverstock. But in the 1990s, a two-core process began with a new tacky resin coverstock (also called reactive urethane) and a new internal weight designed by a computer that could

▶
▶
▶
▶
▶
▶

A History
of the
Bowling
Ball

"prehistoric" stone ball   wooden bowling ball

Bowling Ball!

balance each ball individually. This weight "block" could be spherical, elliptical, light-bulb-shaped, or even a combination of shapes and small counterweights.

Reactive balls gave bowlers more power and hooking punch than ever before. The American Bowling Congress recorded 14,889 perfect games for winter 1991–92. But in 1992–93 when these balls debuted, almost 3,000 more perfect games were bowled (17,654). Some bowlers were unhappy about this. They said those balls made the game too easy. But other bowlers (like you and me) were really, really, really happy.

These days, computers can customize bowling balls with a precise layout of the holes and an exact distribution of the core weight, so that one basic ball can be modified to give this bowler maximum flare, that bowler extra hook, and yet another bowler greater length before hooking. With a ball this personalized, bowlers today concentrate on speed and power rather than accuracy. A customized, reactive ball just grips the last third of the lane, hooks forcefully, plows into "the pocket," and scrambles the pins, even when it's slightly outside the ideal strike zone.

Float-a-Ball

8 lbs

Bowling Alley Science:

A gallon of water weighs 8 pounds. So what? Well, because of the law of displacement, a bowling ball can float! An 8-pound ball takes up more space than 8 pounds of water. Thus a 10-pound ball "hovers," and anything heavier sinks.

10 lbs

14 lbs

rubber bowling ball   polyester bowling ball   urethane-covered bowling ball

You don't need to bowl at a regulation alley, use standard equipment, or join a bowling league. You can improvise a bowling game with household things. Take some inspiration from Pumpkin Bowling. Now, rolling pumpkins at pop bottles isn't exactly an ancient sport that began with the Native Americans explaining the rules to the Pilgrims at the first Thanksgiving. No, it's just your basic tenpin game gone haywire . . . or hay-wagon.

Swap a pumpkin for the bowling ball and plastic pop bottles (filled with sand or water) for the pins. Try miniature pumpkins with one-liter bottles. Try giant squash with detergent jugs. Or, if you have an apple tree, roll a few spotted apples at plastic juice bottles. Or lose the harvest theme and aim snowballs or even old softballs at refilled (and frozen) water bottles. Simply set up a triangle of ten "pins" on your sidewalk or driveway or alley, stand back a few yards, wind up, and heave your "bowling ball" toward the pins.

Speaking of Halloween, check out these clear jack-o'-lantern, skull, and alien balls, where the object appears to float inside the transparent coverstock. The pins might just fall over from fright!

WHAT, DID YOU DRESS IN THE DARK . . . IN A HURRY?

Next time you're at the lanes, check out a pro bowler's shoes. Chances are, they don't match. A right-handed bowler's left shoe has a slippery leather or vinyl sole, while the right shoe has a sticky rubber sole. Why? When the right arm swings forward to deliver the ball, the left shoe slides forward and the right shoe applies the brakes to prevent an accidental step over the line. For left-handed bowlers, the slippery and sticky soles are reversed.

No matter what, their socks should still match.

THE INSIDE SCOOP

The ball's shape is crucial! Balls can't deviate from a sphere by more than 0.001 inch. No more than five holes or grips for holding are permitted. (There are many rules pertaining to these, including the placement of small additional vent holes.) One other hole, up to 1.25 inches in diameter, is allowed for balance.

Grips usually include one deep enough to insert the thumb completely and two other holes drilled to customized depths: either (1) the fingertips only; (2) up to the fingers' first joint; or (3) up to the fingers' first two joints. (Of course, a custom ball is drilled specifically for a particular bowler's hand.)

The diameter must be 8.5 inches; up to another 0.095 inch is permitted.

The circumference must be between 26.704 and 27.002 inches. (Each time a ball is resurfaced, a little coating is removed.)

Ball markings must include the manufacturer's name and logo, ball name and serial number, and the USBC logo.

The composition must be a solid non-metallic material.

The ball's weight must be no heavier than 16 pounds; there is no minimum weight.

So Just How Hard Is Hard?

A bowling ball's hardness is gauged by a Durometer, which shows how easily it can be dented. A pointed steel rod is pressed against the ball with ten pounds of pressure for a certain length of time. (The pressure and time vary according to the type of material being tested.) As a comparison: Your wad of chewing gum measures twenty on the scale. A car tire is about fifty. A construction-site hardhat measures seventy-five. Bowling balls must register at least seventy-two. Especially hard Ebonite bowling balls register one hundred—the maximum rating, which is nearly as hard as a diamond.

Designs, flakes, or other particles (when used) must be embedded 0.25 inch below the ball's surface and can't weight more than 0.05 ounce.

Isn't that just Ducky!?

Bowlers play different games around the globe. European ninepin bowlers play with a six-inch ball on asphalt. Canadian fivepin bowlers use a smaller ball and five pins, each worth a different number of points, depending on their placement. British skittles players lob a small four- to six-inch ball through the air, trying to hit stocky pins arranged at the end of an alley that's a third as long as a tenpin alley. (Midway games where you lob softballs at wooden milk bottles are based on this game.) Even in the States, players remain loyal to two other, even more challenging, bowling games.

Candlepin bowling began in Worcester, Massachusetts, in the late 19th century, and it uses a five-inch ball and tall, thin pins. Similarly, duckpin bowling, Baltimore's version, began around 1900, with two baseball players, John McGraw and Wilbert Robinson. The manager at the bowling establishment they owned had some old tenpins trimmed down to use with smaller balls. Why the name "duckpin" bowling? When McGraw saw the ball send the pins flying, he said they resembled a flock of ducks scattering after a hunter's shot.

Today, these two games are mainly played on the East Coast. They share one key difference from tenpins: Players can roll three balls in each frame. It's just that much harder to roll a smaller, lighter ball down the same sixty-foot alley and knock down all ten pins. "Tenpins is a science," players like to say, "but duckpins is a skill."

The idea of the games is the same, but the pins used in skittles, tenpin, duckpin, and candlepin bowling have some striking differences.

skittles

duckpin

candlepin

tenpin

BALL TALK

Here is a rolling roster of ball deliveries from the pokiest to the curviest to the fastest.

creeper: *a very slow ball, the sort that makes the other player go for refreshments*

poodle, channel ball, or gutter ball: *a ball that veers off the lane and into the channel before reaching the pins*

pumpkin: *a ball thrown with the oomph of a pumpkin lying in a patch*

dead ball: *a ball that barely bumps the pins, creating little excitement from either the pins or the bowler*

floater or flat ball: *a ball that moves down the lane without power, spin, or lift*

curve: *a ball that veers toward the pocket (its course resembles one of the parenthesis around these words)*

bender: *a ball that looks as if it's about to fall into the gutter but then breaks back toward the pins*

hook: *a ball that breaks sharply, shifting toward the pocket*

BB, bullet, rocket, or frozen rope: *a ball that careens down the lane with extra speed*

mixer: *a ball with lots of spin and power*

broom ball or sweeper: *a ball with so much spin power that it brushes the pins away*

snow plow: *a strike ball that hits dead-on*

umbrella ball: *a strike in which the pins fan out like an umbrella*

Broken Record Also Breaks Bowling Balls!

Suresh Joachim of Canada set the *Guinness Book of World Records* for most continuous hours bowled—100 hours—in June 2005. Oh, and he broke a few bowling balls, too.

Million-Dollar Don

Who: "Mr. Bowling," Don Carter of St. Louis, Missouri

Record (after record after record): Don was the first bowler to win all the major tenpin tournaments: the All-Star, the World's Invitational, the Professional Bowlers Association National, and the American Bowling Congress Masters.

What else?: This Grand Slam bowler was also the very first athlete *in any sport* to receive a million-dollar deal to endorse a product. Ebonite® introduced the Gryo-Balanced® ball with Don's name attached to it.

"Quote-a-Balls"

"One advantage of bowling over golf is that you never lose a bowling ball."

—Don Carter

Big-time "bowlers": (left to right) Stan Musial, Mickey Mantle, Yogi Berra, and Don Carter (sitting)

Don't Look Back

Who: Joe Scrandis of Columbia, Maryland
Record: He scored 175 in his best game.
So...what's so great? Joe bowls *backwards*. He faces the fans—not the pins—walks backward toward the line, and heaves the ball behind him. Don't try this at home! Since plenty of bowlers throw gutter balls even when looking straight at the pins, most alleys won't let you try even a few frames of backwards bowling. Who knows where your ball could end up?

Stack 'Em High!

Who: David Kremer of Waukesha, Wisconsin
Record: He can create a tower of eleven bowling balls, one on top of another without glue, rings, or any sort of stabilizer.

Why in the world? "When I was stacking eight balls, television producers would call and say, 'Can you do nine—and break the record on our show?' Once I had stacked nine, another would call: 'It'd be great if you could do ten...on our show!' Now that I've done eleven, the next show will be asking, 'David, can you stack twelve balls?' Like this is easy, people!"

He's No Quack

Who: Pete Signore of Connecticut
Record: In 1992, Pete bowled a score of 279, the highest in the history of duckpin bowling. (Carole Gittings has held the women's record of 265 since 1973.)
What's so great: In tenpin, thousands of bowlers score twelve strikes and reach that 300-point perfection. But one duckpin ball rarely plows down all ten pins. Duckpin bowlers are usually thrilled with a score over 100. Pros only average between130 and 160.

Look, Ma! Two Hands!

Who: Chaz Dennis of Columbus, Ohio
Record: He's the youngest bowler to shoot a 300 game.
What's So Great: Chaz was exactly ten years, two months, and twenty-seven days old when he scored the perfect game with his two-handed, roll-the-ball-between-the-legs technique.

Go for It!

Q: What's red, white, and blue; is 26-feet long; and is found in Iraq and Afghanistan?

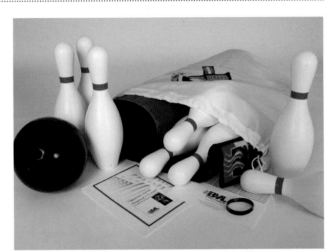

- **a.)** *a portable "Slip 'N Slide" painted with a nifty flag design*
- **b.)** *a trio of camels that do the bunny hop to entertain American troops overseas*
- **c.)** *a portable, all-you-can eat, make-your-own Fourth of July sundae buffet*
- **d.)** *a bowling alley in a bag*

A: **The answer is d.** Bowlers to Veterans Link, bowling's oldest philanthropic group, has shipped more than four hundred bowling kits to American troops throughout the world. Each nylon bag contains a five-pound ball, plastic bowling pins, and scoring sheets. A lane can be assembled or broken down in minutes, so soldiers can relax with a game of tenpins whenever there's a little "peace" and quiet.

In what game are all the other balls out to get this other ball named Jack, who just sits there quietly minding its own business?

The BOCCe Ball!

Pronounce it
~~BOSE, BOH-see, BAHK, BAH-kee~~
BAH-chee!

ACTUAL SIZE!

Some favorite pastimes in times past were sports whose rule book must have simply read: "1. Okay, whoever comes closest to hitting that thing over there wins." (You can't fit a lot of rules on a carved-stone book.) Various ball-tossing games included teammates, obstacles, boundaries, and limits on how or where to throw the ball, but they all involved competitors trying to accurately and strategically pitch one or more balls a short distance toward another target.

Thank the Egyptians for inventing mummies, marshmallows, and also the first bocce-like game (around 5,000 BC), in which players lobbed polished stones at other stones. That contest skipped across the Mediterranean Sea into the Old World, becoming the varied sports we now know as bowling, croquet, billiards, golf, marbles, and bocce. (Actually, there's good reason to think that most ball games claim the same few ancestors.)

Early Greek physicians prescribed a version of bocce as a "restorative activity." Very, very roughly translated, those doctors' advice today would be: "Come on! Get off the computer, go outside, and toss some balls at other balls! Fresh air will do you good!"

Romans also enjoyed such games, tossing coconuts that had been transported from Africa along with elephants and rhinos who, it goes without

Lignum vitae (a.k.a. ironwood) is both hard and beautiful.

saying, were definitely not for tossing. Once the Romans created tools that were sharp, they gave their fingernails a good manicure and started carving balls from the hard wood of local olive trees.

As ships began to travel easily to the West Indies, the lignum vitae, a tree with the hardest wood on the planet, became the first choice of ball carvers, who eagerly turned the imported wood into bowling-, billiard-, and bocce balls, as well as new ship masts for still more trips to the West Indies to pick up still more lignum vitae.

Today, the balls for bocce and its relatives are made from hard plastics, custom cast for each sport. Throughout the world, these games are played on beaches, lawns, gravel courts, and even frozen lakes. In Belgium alone, players can specialize in games that use lopsided balls (called bowls) including *krulbol* (curled bowls), *platte bol* (flat bowls), *ronde bol* (round bowls), *gaaibol* (jay bowls), *putbol* (pit bowls—not to be confused with pit bulls, which are not Belgian and are really hard to roll), *vloerbol* (floor bowls), and *bakbol* (tray bowls). For all the variations, these games share one other appealing trait: unlike many sports, they can be enjoyed by people of any age and any skill level. If you've never played bocce, it's high time you gave it a shot—or a roll!

THE INSIDE SCOOP

Bocce

Bocce, the third-most-played sport in the world, is a team event where players roll the balls from a crouched position. The court, made of hard dirt or clay, has low wooden sides that allow for bank shots.

Composition *is a hard synthetic plastic with identifying colors or marks. Each game includes 8 balls—4 balls in each of two patterns or colors.*

The jack *is called the* pallino *(Italian for "little marble"). It's made of wood or plastic and has a diameter between 1.375 and 2.5 inches.*

The ball's weight *is 2.2 pounds.*

The ball's diameter *is 4.5 inches.*

No bias! *These balls must be perfectly round and roll without curving.*

Petanque

Petanque (*French, pey-TAHNK*) is a team sport usually played on a 36 x 12-foot field of grass, gravel, or sand. Players toss the ball from a standing position, feet fixed in place—or, in French, *pieds tanqués*, from which the word petanque is derived.

All competition balls *must be metal. They can't be weighted, sanded, or modified after manufacturing.*

No bias! *These balls must be perfectly round and roll without curving.*

The jack *is called the* cochonnet *(French for "piglet"). It can be wood or plastic and any color. The diameter is between .98 inch and 1.38 inches; the weight is not critical.*

The ball's weight *must be between 1.43 and 1.76 pounds and clearly stated on the ball, along with the manufacturer's name. (Youth competitions use 1.32-pound balls.)*

The ball's diameter *must be between 2.77 and 3.15 inches.*

Lawn Bowls
or Flat Green Bowls

Teams play lawn bowls back and forth in one direction on a green that's between 33 and 44 yards long and bordered with a ditch. Like golfers choosing different clubs for specific situations, bowlers choose different woods in their set according to what action they want: roll straight, right curve, left curve.

Composition is of plastic resin. These balls are called "woods," not in an attempt to confuse you and me, but because they used to be carved from lignum vitae.

The jack is usually white, weighs 10 ounces, and has a maximum diameter of 2.5 inches.

The ball's weight is between 2.5 pounds to 3.5 pounds.

The ball's diameter is between 4.5 to 5.125 inches. Each bowl is marked to state how it's biased: flatter on one side and slightly heavier on the opposite side. As the wood slows before coming to a stop, it curves more.

BALL TALK

In bocce, players have a few throwing options, depending on their skill level and where the game balls are positioned on the field.

puntata: *On a smooth surface with few balls in the way, players gently roll the ball from a crouched position. Most amateurs play the game with this shot alone.*

volo: *This is bocce's flying shot, thrown underhand or overhand. Skilled players shoot this ball high, adding reverse spin on the release (as a pitcher does with a curveball), so that the ball lands accurately and sticks in position.*

raffa: *This is a running shot in which players run a few steps, fire the ball underhand or overhand, and follow through with a few more steps. It's a* "smash" *shot, thrown close to the ground with the goal of moving other balls on the field.*

gelato: *Neither as large nor as hard as a bocce ball, gelato (or Italian ice cream) is more refreshing after a long game of all that rolling, shooting, and running.*

SinkaBall

What if you tossed into an aquarium six regulation-size bocce balls, each made of a different material:

- **mahogany**
- **lignum vitae (remember this stuff?)**
- **balsa wood**
- **foil wrappers from Hershey's Kisses®️ crumpled together really, really tightly**
- **gold**
- **maple**

Which would float and which would sink?

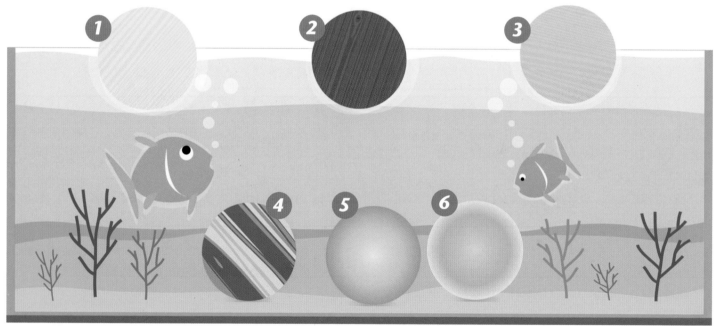

The first thing you will notice is that three of your balls float and three of them sink. The floaters are **#1** balsa wood, one of the lightest woods in the world; **#2** mahogany, which is often used to make nice furniture; and **#3** maple, the reason pancakes are happy. But why do they float?

If your aquarium was a one-square-foot cube, the water inside would weigh 62.5 pounds. One square foot of balsa wood weighs 6.25 pounds; mahogany, 45 pounds; and maple, 47 pounds. Since these woods all **weigh less** than an equal amount of water, they float.

The sinkers are the balls made of substances **heavier** than water. *Lignum vitae*, **#4**, is a wood like the other three floaters,

but a one-square-foot cube of it would weigh 88 pounds—25.5 more pounds than water. Your Hershey's Kiss foil ball, **#5**, is a very light metal, aluminum foil, but a compressed square foot of it weighs 168 pounds. And a one-square-foot cube of **#6**, gold, a very heavy metal, would weigh 1,206 pounds.*

*No wonder people have found better things to do with gold than heaving big balls of it across the lawn—especially since a set of bocce balls would cost you more than a quarter billion dollars! (The price of gold fluctuates, let's use an average of $650 an ounce. So, a solid gold bocce ball would weigh 33.27 pounds, or 532.32 ounces, times $650 an ounce, equals $346,008, times 8 balls in a set, equals $2,768,064.)

ABSOLUTELY MARBLE-OUS!
Aggies, Peawees, Cat's Eyes, and Bumboozers

Along with Egyptians and Romans (but not in the same circles drawn on the ground), ancient Aztecs, Native Americans, and the Japanese all played miniature forms of bocce. Each culture created its own small spheres—some used china, glass, clay, flint, semi-precious stones such as agates and jasper, or, as the name suggests, bits of marble.

With swirled or corkscrew centers, flecked or spiral surfaces, embedded figurines or patterns, handmade or machine-made, the marble, more than any other ball, has invited individual craftsmanship, decoration, ingenuity, and, not far behind, collectors! What's more, there are almost as many marble games as there are types of marbles!

Believe it or not, seventy-five years ago, West Virginia was the marble-making capital of the known universe. Of the eighteen marble factories, all but four were located in West Virginia where glass workers, railroads, and natural gas were all available. One of the nation's oldest, Peltier Glass in Illinois, produced a record 141 million marbles in 1954—the very year in which the author of this book was born. Coincidence? Absolutely!

But in the late 1950s, Japan and Taiwan entered the marble market with less-expensive marbles. (How "less expensive" could marbles get? Kids were already buying a sack of twenty marbles for a dime at the toy store.) Today the vast majority of the world's marbles are made in Mexico, while individual glass artists continue to create marvels of transparency and color collected by museums and folks who have lost their marbles everywhere.

As for the sport itself? There's nothing "kiddie" about the many tournaments and championship games held each year in countries such as England, Germany, and the Czech Republic. Even in America, marbles' popularity is growing—and this time, it's for keepsies*!

*Keepsies, or "playing for keeps," is where players keep any of their opponents' marbles they've won. The opposite? "Funsies," or "playing for fun," where players return one another's marbles after each game.

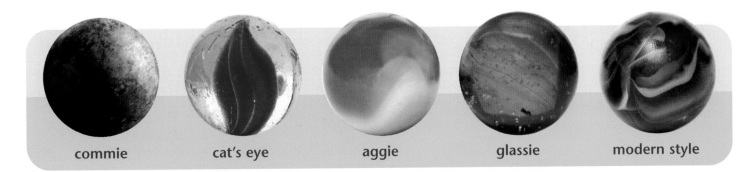

commie   cat's eye   aggie   glassie   modern style

BALL TALK

What's in <u>Your</u> Marble Bag?

Most games include one larger shooter, known as the taw (particularly large shooters are called bumboozers, bumbos, or bowlers, and they often are as large as an inch in diameter), and target balls, typically .675 of an inch in diameter, known as mibs, kimmies, or ducks. Marbles with a diameter smaller than half an inch, are called peewees (or peawees). But it's the composition and coloring of your marbles that really gets the "ball talk" rolling.

glassie, milkie, and purie: These are the simplest glass marbles. Made in any one color, glassies are clear, milkies are translucent and usually white, and puries are opaque.

cat's eye: This is a clear marble with a vane of color stretching thought the center. Many variations in color and patterns abound in these marbles, which were first produced in Japan in the 1950s.

commie: This was a glazed clay marble. In the early twentieth century, ceramic marbles were a thousand times more common—hence, the name—than glass marbles. (You could buy thirty commies for a penny, but one glassie would cost you between two cents and a nickel.)

crockies: They are fancier relatives of commies, made of stoneware and glazed, and include chinas, which are made from porcelain, a harder, finer clay.

aggie: Originally derived from the word "agate," these are marbles made from this natural mineral. (Among marble fans, the word now refers to any marble.)

immies: are imitation agates: clear glass streaked with color to resembles the agate's pattern.

end of day: This is a one-of-a-kind marble that glass workers would make from all the leftover bits of glass after a long of day of production. These especially colorful, randomly speckled marbles were often given to neighborhood kids. When the glass flecks stretch and swirl around a core, the marble resembles—and is called—an onionskin.

fried marble: This is a marble that's intentionally crackled by dropping very hot marbles into cold water and then heating them again to seal the cracks. No two are ever alike.

DO TRY THIS AT HOME: Stir-Fried Marbles

Feeling a little stir crazy? On the verge of cracking up? Then delve into the world of marble-making! But because the creating of a glass marble would have you working in front of an 1800°F furnace, I've got two other ideas for you. First, you can pretend to be a pioneer kid on the Great Plains. No general store within miles, no chance to order things through the Pony Express, so you and your friends can make marbles from cow manure. (There should be plenty around, since it's used as heating fuel in pioneer homes.) The pioneers actually had no special technique, so just roll bits of manure into marble-sized balls. Let dry in the sun until hard.

Okay, you might like my second idea better: Create your own unique crackle marbles that catch the light and sparkle.

The original recipe involved frying marbles in a skillet, but with today's technology, we've got three safer options. Essentially, you'll be stressing the glass by suddenly changing its temperature, causing the marble to crack just like an ice cube does when you pour a warm beverage over it. A glass artist does just the opposite—once a marble is finished, they anneal the hot glass, which means to gradually cool and strengthen the object by slowly lowering its temperature in a special oven.

You'll need:
- clear marbles (new ones can be found at hobby or craft stores)
- a grown-up to help—the marbles will be hot!
- oven mitts (oh, and an oven!)
- an aluminum pie tin or empty coffee can
- a large bowl of ice

The Oven Method
- Bake the marbles in the disposable aluminum pie tin or empty coffee can for 20 minutes at 275°F.
- Place a large bowl of ice water nearby.
- When 20 minutes are up, have an adult remove the metal container using oven mitts.
- Dump the marbles into the ice bath.
- Leave them chilling for 15 minutes.

The Freezer/Teapot Method
- Let your marbles have a sleepover in the freezer.
- In the morning, have a grown-up bring a teapot of water to the boil.
- Put the frozen marbles in an empty coffee can or other metal container.
- Carefully dump in the boiling water.
- Let the marbles chill for 15 minutes.

The Microwave Method
- Put a few marbles in a microwave-safe bowl.
- Microwave for 2 minutes.
- Using oven mitts, remove the bowl from the microwave.
- The marbles will crack as they cool from the inside out.
- Be patient! Do not touch the marbles for at least 1 hour. If they didn't crack enough, increase the time on your next batch. (Do not use the already microwaved marbles!)

*No—your marbles won't pop like popcorn. Honest!

Now that your "fried marbles" have cooled, check out some marble games. Or turn them into beads and make jewelry. (Craft stores carry bell caps—which are like the tops of acorns—that you can glue on your marbles. Each has a loop, so a crackled marble can be strung on a keychain, a necklace chain, or other dangling thingie.)

Marble Madness

One Major Mibster

Who: Cathy Runyan-Svacina of Kansas City, Missouri

Record: With more than a million marbles in her possession (the number fluctuates since she's always trading, buying, selling, and giving away her marbles), "The Marble Lady" also holds the record for hosting the largest marble tournament, pitting 569 mibsters against one another!

Okay, so what's a mibster? They're sort of like mobsters and monsters and ministers in that they're people, but since the root word, mib, is the Latin word for "marble," mibsters only go after other marble players.

While we're playing with words: A mibologist is a marble expert. So he or she has all of his or her marbles when it comes to the history and facts about these spheres.

Go Figure!

Who: Some of the most unusual collectibles are sulfides (or sulphides) or figure marbles: clear glass surrounding a tiny carving such as a porcupine, child playing croquet, Beethoven, gargoyle, Mother Goose, mummy, Santa Claus on a potty, or even a squirrel with a nut. The figures are created in porcelain, a clay that can be heated to the same temperature as molten glass.

What else: These marbles weren't intended to be flicked at other marbles in the ring. They were baby gifts! (Huh? Like choking wasn't a problem in the nineteenth century?) And, for the record, sulfides have nothing to do with sulfur, from which the name arose—by mistake.

Cyber★Marble Miscellany

What: Some of the smallest marbles you can get your fingers on.

Where: www.landofmarbles.com –A site for collectors, it presents a huge resource on marble varieties, versions of marble games, news on competitions and innovations, plus all the lingo and lore of the game.

Where: www.marblemuseum.org – A Web site with a gallery of marbles from around the world and throughout history, with articles on many types of marble making processes and games.

What: Some of the oldest marbles in America—and lots of great marble mania.

"Quote★a★Ball"

"I regard golf as an expensive way of playing marbles."
—*G. K. Chesterton*

What ball is hit from the ground like a golf ball, slides through more hoops than a basketball, bounces off other balls like a billiard ball, but is played with the slow strategies of chess?

LOOK!

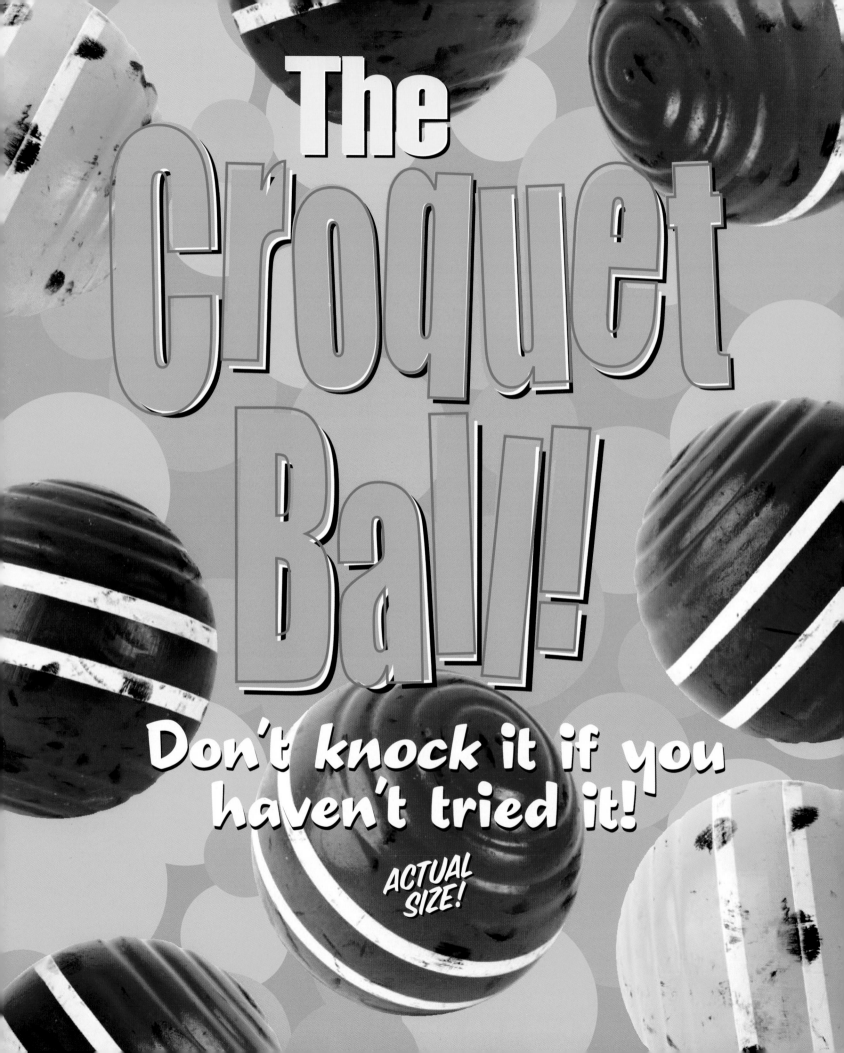

The Croquet Ball!

Don't knock it if you haven't tried it!

ACTUAL SIZE!

n the 14th century, shepherds in Southern France were bored enough that they used their crooks (which they called *croches*) to knock wooden balls through hoops they crafted from bent willow branches and poked into the ground. They liked to call the game *Paille Maille*, although *croche* may be how we got the name "croquet." After the game crossed the English Channel, the British spelled the game Pele Mele or Pall Mall, but the Irish preferred the name Crooky, from the Gaelic word *cluiche* (pronounced "crooky"), meaning "play," which also could have been the root of our word "croquet." (If you're confused, so are most of the croquet historians!)

By the late 19th century, the game, commonly called croquet, became the most widely played sport in England, partly because women were welcomed outdoors with the men! After dinner, ladies and gentlemen often competed against one another—with a chaperone, because if a ball "accidentally" rolled behind a hedge, the game could provide a chance for courting couples to kiss. (How wicket! I mean, wicked!)

Soon fashionable croquet courts were being created from ground-up cockleshells, and the hoops—large enough for a cocker spaniel to crawl through—were decorated with flowers. Pretty fancy for a sport, no?

Over in the States, the game was eagerly embraced by President Rutherford B. Hayes, who really didn't care about where the word croquet came from! He spent six whole dollars of government funds to buy a "good quantity" of croquet balls, which his critics proclaimed was "an outrageous expense." The President repaid the country from his personal piggybank. Meanwhile, croquet became the first sport in which both men and women competed together. By 1900, U.S. players created new rules for the game, establishing a standardized court size, reducing the size of the wickets, and halving the number of balls from eight to four.

Even to this day, the sport continues to inspire wacky ideas (You'll see when you read the end of this chapter!), although nothing is likely to top Lewis Carroll's version in *Alice's Adventures in Wonderland*, created almost 150 years ago.

"Alice thought she had never seen such a curious croquet-ground in her life; it was all ridges and furrows; the balls were live hedgehogs, the mallets live flamingoes, and the soldiers had to double themselves up and to stand on their hands and feet, to make the arches."

—from *Alice's Adventures in Wonderland*

THE INSIDE SCOOP

The core of *competition croquet balls is compressed cork. (Solid wooden or plastic balls are often used for backyard games.)*

The outer surface *is solid plastic. Most competition balls are milled with two sets of about fifty shallow grooves that evenly cover the surface.*

The diameter *is 3.625 inches. (A wicket's height is 12 inches above the ground, but its width is only 0.125 of an inch wider than the ball.)*

The ball's weight *is one pound with a quarter of an ounce leeway on either side.*

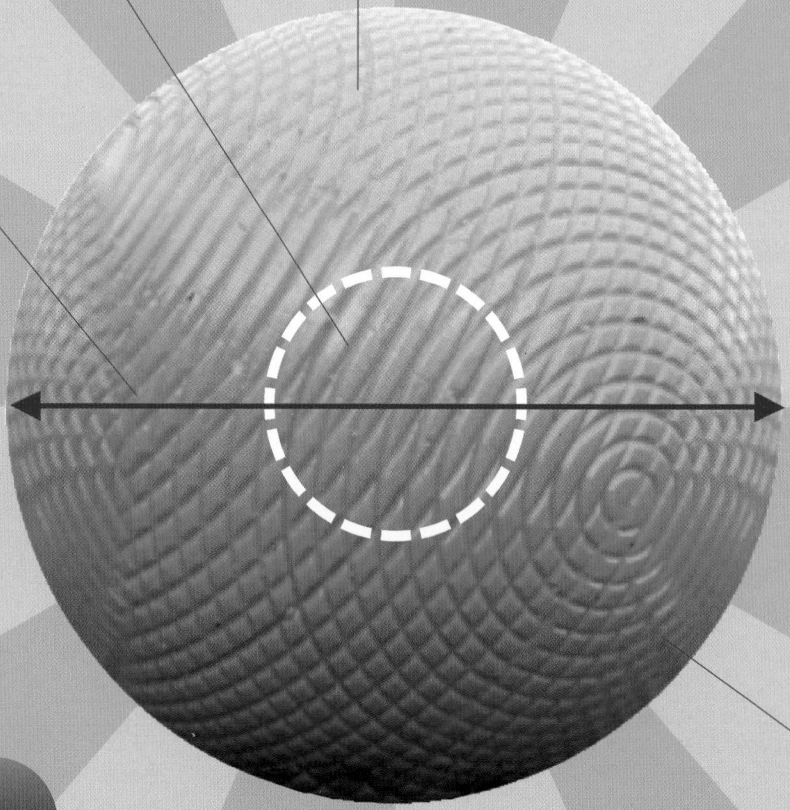

Colors
Four solid colors— blue, red, black, and yellow— are used in all competition games. Green and orange are also used in recreational play.

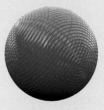

5'

30-45"

Bounce-ablity
When dropped from a height of 5 feet onto a 2-inch-thick steel plate framed in concrete, balls must rebound between one half and three quarters of the total distance (or between 30 and 45 inches). Within any set of balls, any ball's bounce height can't vary by more than 3 inches.

BALL TALK

roquet: ("row-KAY") to hit your ball against another ball, sending it rolling and giving you the chance for bonus strokes.

peel: a stroke that sends another's ball through a wicket.

rush shot: a ball that's traveled a good distance along its targeted path.

blob: a ball that doesn't clear a wicket and sticks in its jaws.

rover: once a ball has run through the last hoop, it becomes a rover ball (and in the game of Poison or Snake, the poison ball).

spoon: using the mallet to shove the ball across the grass, rather than strike it—clop—into action.

Aunt Emma: a player with no offensive strategy whatsoever, who simply takes one hoop at a time, boring all opponents into quitting early.

War Games

During World War II, croquet balls were enlisted in the Allied war effort. In Operation Post-Box, Major Clayton Hutton of the British Military Intelligence worked with toy and sporting-goods manufacturers to devise ". . . a variety of hiding-places, carving out secret caches in the handles of table tennis bats, in chess men, and in the wooden frame of the board, in dominoes, in Indian clubs, in skittles, in cricket balls, in darts and in dart boards, in drum sticks . . ."

Allied prisoners would receive a coded letter clueing them into the disguised items. Prison guards would overlook these packages since prisoners were permitted packages from the Red Cross or family members. But inside, a map would be sandwiched within a board game, a tool slid into a cricket bat, a saw built into a comb, a tiny compass tucked inside a ring-toss game, or a map or money folded inside a hollow croquet ball. Some 35,000 troops escaped before the war's end, in no small part because of these "war games."

No Rest for the Wicket:
Croquet for Every Sort of Lawn

Knocking balls through narrow targets arranged in specific patterns becomes totally different games depending on the terrain, the number of competitors and their skill level, and the quantity of sugary, caffeinated beverages the players downed before the game. Each of the popular games below is scored differently and has unique rules about the order in which shots must be taken and the layouts of the wickets on the lawn.

American or Six-Wicket Croquet

Your team and the opposing team must maneuver balls through a course of wickets and finally strike the stake. Hitting another ball and/or sending your ball through a wicket will earn you another shot. Any ball that's hit becomes "dead" until another ball makes it "live" again by being sending it through a wicket. In this game, great strategy wins more games than shot-making skill.

International or Association Rules Croquet

Your mission in this competition is to run two balls through each of six hoops two times in a specific order and end by hitting the center peg. "Taking croquet" is key in this game: Hit another ball with one of your balls (making a roquet!), and

you get two additional strokes. How? Place your ball against the ball you just struck and whack them both forward (that's taking croquet), thereby advancing your own balls or thwarting an opponent's progress. Then, you get another stroke with your ball, unless one of the balls went foul on your last hit. Great players develop many techniques and strategies to build these extra strokes; the best can send a second ball through a hoop (that's called "peeling") along with their hit ball or can run through all twelve hoops in a single turn.

Rock around the Croq

The first croquet balls were simply polished stones or lumps of clay.

French shepherds created balls from tanned animal hides stuffed with feathers, from ivory, or from willow branches.

In the early 20th century, the Jaques sporting-goods company carved one-piece wooden balls from "the finest Turkish boxwood," so their ads proclaimed.

Golf or Obstacle Croquet

In this game, each wicket is like the hole on a miniature golf course. You and your friends all shoot for one wicket at the same time, hoping to be the first through. (Only the first ball through each wicket scores the point.) The player who reaches seven points wins and heads to the kitchen to bring the other players their choice of lemonade or ice tea. This game is easily adapted to backyards and parks and lends itself to creative, and even goofy, course design with lots of inconvenient traps, trees, and slopes.

Backyard Croquet or Nine-Wicket Croquet

This informal version has so many variations you and your friends should always agree on the "house rules" before the game starts. Basically, it's six balls, two wooden stakes, and seven wire wickets positioned in a double-diamond configuration. You are playing against every other player, hoping to score the fourteen wicket points and two stakes points for each of your two balls. Pass through a wicket, hit a stake or another ball, and bonus points are yours. Or you can decide that the first ball that clears all the hoops—the rover ball—becomes poison! Any ball it hits is out of the game. But if your ball roquets a poison ball, or if the poison ball goes through a wicket, your ball goes out of the game. Whoever has the last ball on the field is the winner.

Next, Jaques created composition balls: a solid core, a layer of compressed cork, and an outer plastic coating (polyurethane) milled with grooves. Only one problem: In the hot sun, these balls expanded and barely fit through the wickets!

The hollow balls we use today arrived. A mold with one pound of composition material was placed in a centrifuge and spun. This concentrated the ball's weight to the outside and left a hollow center. These balls slid across the lawn when struck and then somersaulted into a roll.

Inventors continue to mold balls with new types of nylon and polyurethane and to press or mill different groove patterns to refine the ball's performance.

Croquet for Cuckoos
and Other Loony Creatures

As you've seen, croquet is a whole lot easier than batting hedgehog-balls with a flamingo-mallet. However, for whatever reason, players seem particularly eager to take this simple, cheerful backyard game and ramp it up into an oversized, perilous, and outlandish event.

In Mondo Croquet players dress in Alice costumes and use sledge hammers to move bowling balls around a huge figure-8 course. In the 1970s, players even created a mega-mondo version called "Guerilla Croquet," in which players drove trucks with huge tires to knock six-foot-diameter balls through enormous wickets.

There's also Toequet, which involves players kicking soccer balls through oversized wickets on a somewhat larger course.

You don't need a mallet to play kickball croquet—just a good strong foot!

Bicycle Croquet—or *Fahrradkrocket* as it's known by its Austrian inventors—puts two players on bicycles (no training wheels allowed, although a player may compete on a unicycle). Taking turns with their mallets, players have ten seconds to hit croquet balls through a course of wickets without letting any part of their body touch the ground.

Finally, there's eXtreme Croquet, a game open to a great deal of freedom and potential silliness. The course is laid out on anything but a well-manicured lawn. Wickets are spread out across large distances and placed on ice, in creeks, among tree roots, or in mud—or, why not?—puddles of chocolate pudding.

Anyone for a wintry round of wicked-cold croquet? Can you imagine a more "extreme" teeth-chattering game than knocking ice-cold croquet balls outside the National Oceanic & Atmospheric Administration Observatory . . . at the S-S-S-S-South P-P-Pole?

BALL of FAME

THE BIG MAC HIMSELF

Who: Robert Fulford of Great Britain

Record: He's the only player to have played on six teams that have won the MacRobertson International Trophy. Robert has won sixty-one tournament matches and lost only three out of twenty-nine singles matches. He's also the current—and five-time—Croquet World Champion.

What's so great: Held every four years, the "Mac Shield" is croquet's Stanley Cup or Super Bowl. Six players from Great Britain, Australia, New Zealand, and the United States all compete in a round robin of matches. Since joining the four-country competition in 1993, the U.S. has only placed third three times and fourth twice.

"QUOTE·A·BALL"

"Croquet is like pool, except you're standing on the table."

—Jerry "The Barbarian" Stark, five-time U.S. Croquet Association title holder

CROQUET ROOKIE

Who: Jacques Fournier of Phoenix, Arizona

Record: When he was twelve, Jacques became the youngest player to enter the U.S. National Croquet Championship. He took fourth place and the title, Rookie of the Year.

What else is so great: Jacques is also the first American and youngest player ever to compete in the final round of the British Open. He's one of three players in the sport's history to leave the World Croquet Championships undefeated. And he represented the USA on two Mac Shield teams.

What ball do you hold in one hand, hope will travel as far as possible, but try never to throw? LOOK!

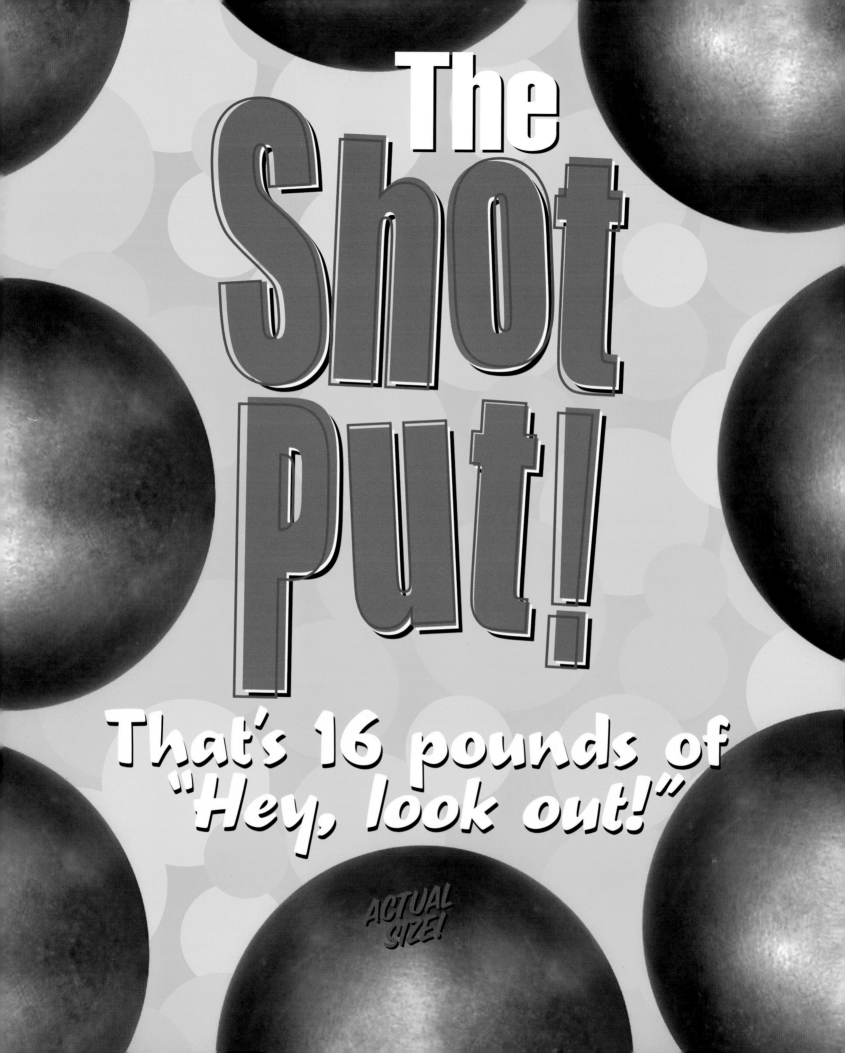

"**S**hot" is another word for a cannonball; "put" is another word for thrust. Throwing a 16- or even an 8-pound sphere of iron as you would a baseball is another word for OUCH! Throwing an object that heavy usually tears, bursts, or breaks something in your arm.

Humans have been heaving heavy things through the air for 2,000 years—at least. Celtic men, as they cleared the craggy ground that would become Ireland and Scotland, or while they waited for a local doughnut shop to open (or for doughnuts to be invented, for that matter) couldn't help testing their strength against one another. The words, "Betcha I can throw this farther than you can," must be among the first words spoken in any language.

Some of these ancient games continue to this day. The *clachneart* (Scottish for "stone of strength") was the original shot-put competition in which players hurled rocks the size and weight of modern shot puts.

So when did athletes start heaving metal balls? During the Middle Ages, soldiers had a little down time, history suggests, and hurled iron cannon balls. And while modern shot puts now come in a variety of weights and materials, these changes haven't changed the competition the way innovations in baseball covers or bowling-ball cores have radically affected those games.

Using only one hand and either gliding, spinning, or hopping across a circle seven feet in diameter, a shot putter pushes the ball as if delivering an uppercut to a punching bag: a speedy up-out-and-over burst of power. Sure, arm strength is everything, but technique is everything else: Legs supply most of the ball's speed, the wind-up turn creates momentum, and the footwork kicks up the propulsion. To win a meet, a "thrower" (I know, I know, but that's what they're called) shoves three balls from the shoulder-chin position, hoping that the farthest ball will outdistance the competitors' best throws.

Some shot puts today are cast iron, while others are brass or stainless steel turned on a machine. Lighter balls are designed for younger or Special Olympic athletes. Shot puts geared for indoor use usually have a hard rubber shell. Practice ones usually have a rougher coating and extra pounds to help players strengthen their grip.

The hammer throw uses a shot put on a cable with a handle. Athletes in this event twirl the hammer as they spin around and try not to get dizzy, finally launching the weight over the shoulder.

In this chapter, sharing the field with this heavy fistful of metal, we'll toss around a dozen or so less ancient "balls" that have inspired new competitions. Even if they never become Olympic events, they certainly prove one point: Human beings just have to throw things!

THE INSIDE SCOOP

The composition
is either solid metal—iron, stainless steel, brass, or any other metal that's at least as hard as brass—or a shell of metal filled with lead. A polyurethane cover, often brightly colored, can add a final layer. Indoor shot puts have a hard rubber exterior so the gym won't look as if a meteor shower came along to pummel the floor during recess.

The ball's surface is smooth—it has no textures or grooves for gripping.

The diameter is 4.5 inches (men) or 4 inches (women). Some competitions permits a small leeway on either side to allow for a player's hand size and grip.

The ball's weight is 16 pounds for men. For women, the ball weighs just over half as much: 8.8 pounds.

4.5 inches

Incoming!

Since shot puts aren't found like stones on the side of the road, people in every land find other things to hurl so that they can feel that special Olympic-shot-putter feeling. (You've probably had that urge some mornings waiting for the bus.) And some of these objects aren't even remotely ball-like! If you travel this big ball of a globe, you can compete in events where you can toss pizzas, brooms, pancakes, pumpkins, toilets, cow chips, cell phones, eggs, barrels, popcorn, fish, watermelons, cheese, and skillets—to name just a few of my favorites.

"I'm sorry, did you say cow chips?"

Yes, tossing cow chips (or cow patties) is popular in places where, well, where cows poop. But let's moooo-ve on. Here are some record throws in the field of some more unusual "shots."

1. **regular old car tire**–42 feet (Brian Oldfield, USA)
2. **shot put**–75 feet, 10.5 inches (Randy Barnes, USA)
3. **frozen whole tuna**–122.14 feet (Sean Carlin, Australia)
4. **2-pound fruitcake**–124 feet (Sean Hall, USA)
5. **billiard cue**–141 feet, 4 inches (Dan Kornblum, Germany)
6. **regular old house brick**–148 feet, 6 inches (Dave Wattle, United Kingdom)
7. **rolling pin**–175 feet, 5 inches (Lori La Deane Adams, USA)
8. **70-mph human cannonball**–185 feet, 10 inches (David "Cannonball" Smith Sr., USA)
9. **cow chip** (approximately 1 pound)–266 feet (Steve Urner, USA)
10. **cell phone**–291.99 feet (Lassi Etelatalo, a Finnish javelin thrower)
11. **baseball**–445 feet, 10 inches (Glen Gorbous, Canada)

BALL of FAME

Far Flung

Who: Randy Barnes of Charleston, WV

Record: At the 1996 Olympics, Randy took the gold with a throw of 75 feet, 10.25 inches—2 feet farther than any other competitor. The women's world record—74 feet, 3 inches—is held by Natalya Lisovskaya of Moscow.

What else: One way an athlete trains for this event is by lifting very heavy weights many times and really fast. A shot put feels light as a feather compared to that!

Give it Your Best Shot

Who: Milan Roskopf of Slovakia

Record: Considered the inventor of this sport, Milan holds the record for juggling three 16-pound shot puts for 52 seconds.

What else: The original "power juggler," Milan's records also include juggling three 6.6-pound balls for 7 minutes, 7 seconds; three 11-pound balls for 1 minute, 35 seconds; three 18.7-pound balls for 39.5 seconds; and three 22-pound balls for 15.8 seconds.

What balls do you have to break before you can even start the game? LOOK!

The Billiard Ball!

Everybody into the pool!

ACTUAL SIZE!

n the very, *very* beginning, pool (a.k.a.: billiards) was an outdoor sport. (In the very, *very* beginning, there were no "indoors," of course.) A lawn worked as a pool table, crooked sticks served as cues, and small rocks were the "natural" choice for balls. (Yes, dodo eggs were rounder, but they made better omelets than rocks.) In that "stone age," games of pool were as much like croquet or golf as they were like pool. (Remember, back far enough, the roots of these games tangle together.)

When pool was finally invited inside, it left its muddy boots at the door, the "lawn" became a grass-colored tablecloth, carved wooden balls replaced the stone balls, and each player brought along a crooked wooden stick with a broad head, called a mace, to shove, rather than jab, the balls. Because balls kept falling off the edge, shallow gutters—think of a moat around a castle—were added to the tables. (Bumpers that keep the ball in play were still years off.)

Along about 1600 AD, the name "billiard" stuck to the sport. It's French, from *bille*, meaning "ball," and *art*, suggesting the art of play. *Cue* is French, for "tail"; players started flipping the mace around to the *tail* end when a ball was trapped at the table's edge. (And while we're taking French lessons, "pool" comes from the French word *poule*, a kind of wagering in which all players put money into a pot that's then divided among the winners.)

Today hundreds of ball games are played on tables worldwide. The three main sports are pocket billiards, which include the popular games of 8-ball, 9-ball, and straight pool; carom (pool without pockets); and snooker, which is played with fifteen red balls and six colored balls, in addition to the white cue ball. Even though table size, table covering, cue length, and ball size and color vary slightly among the different contests, the goal of these games is pretty much to hit other balls (called object balls) with a wooden stick (called a stick) in hopes of moving them into pockets (called—okay, I guess you get the idea) or bouncing them off as many bumpers as possible. And the goal of every parent who has a pool table in the game room is for you and your friends to keep your potato chips and pop bottles off the table! Come on!

Sometimes you just don't want to get out of the pool to play a good game of pool.

The Elephant in the Pool Room and Other Problems

Before arriving on America shores in the early nineteenth century, the wooden pool ball took a 275-year wrong turn: to Africa and to India where balls could be made from elephant tusks. Aside from bringing these great beasts to the edge of extinction, ivory pool balls posed innumerable troubles: They had to dry for two years, and they still cracked, split, and eventually warped. Carvers preferred small tusks from female African elephants in order to make balls of uniform weight and size, so each rack of balls took the lives of two elephants. (Ivory balls were outlawed in 1970.)

As the cost of ivory soared, in 1863, Brunswick, a New York table maker, offered a vast sum of money—$10,000—for an ivory substitute. Folks proposed hollow steel balls, balls made of Crystalate (ground-up cow bones), and even balls molded of ivory dust and shellac. Finally, a chemist experimenting with nitrocellulose, a compound used to make gunpowder, cooked up a thermoplastic: a substance that could molded with heat and pressure and then cooled into a hard substance. Composed of Celluloid—the material used to make movie film as well as dozens of things from purses to silverware handles—this new pool ball was perfect. Oh, except it did have one tiny problem: When two balls collided (kind of the whole point of pool, right?), they could explode, burst into flames, and generally ruin everyone's good time.

About the time the late nineteenth century brought electric lights—and, consequently, a cooler, easier-to-breathe-in, and brighter pool room—plastic balls were developed that didn't require pool players to duck or cover their eyes after each shot. By 1935, modern balls composed of solid resin were standard.

Made from the same substance as gasoline, nylon hosiery, candle wax, and Zip-lock bags, pools balls begin as crude oil. As oil is heated and cooled, it "cracks" into components, which are then mixed and heated with other chemicals under further pressure to create a substance with many, many bonds between its component elements—polymers. Plastic is large molecules made of smaller molecules chemically bonded together—and it can be molded, pressed, squeezed, or (in the case of pool balls) cast into perfect 2.5-inch spheres.

A set of vintage billiard balls

"quote·a·ball"

About billiards: ". . . a health-inspiring, scientific game, lending recreation to the otherwise fatigued mind."

—*Abraham Lincoln,
the sixteenth president of the United States*

THE INSIDE SCOOP

The ball's surface *must be unpolished and wax-free, but it also should be dust- and oil-free.*

As for composition, *billiard balls are cast from phenolic resin, a very hard plastic.*

A pocket billiard ball weighs *between 5.5 and 6 ounces. Snooker and carom balls weigh slightly more.*

The ball's shape *is a perfect sphere. Each billiard ball is molded and finished so that it's utterly balanced, whether moving or at rest.*

The diameter *is 2.5 inches, with a tiny leeway of 0.005 inches. Snooker and carom balls are larger.*

Not actual size

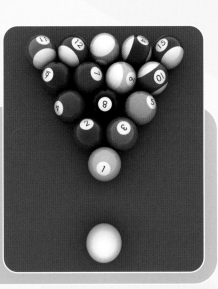

Every set of balls must include one white cue ball and fifteen color-coded and numbered object balls. The numbers are printed twice, each on opposites sides of the ball. Solid-color balls (solids) are numbered so that 1=yellow, 2=blue, 3=red, 4=purple, 5=orange, 6=green, 7=maroon, and 8=black. The white balls with color bands (stripes) are numbered so that 9=yellow band, 10=blue band, 11=red band, 12=purple band, 13=orange band, 14=green band, and 15=maroon band.

winning Spinning

Pool players don't merely poke the stick at the cue ball and hope it will bang into some ball, any ball, that will ricochet somewhere and end up somewhere else. Like a tennis player serving, a pitcher winding up to throw, or a golfer lining up a putt, a billiard pro wants to predict the ball's entire path to the goal.

Along with controlling how much force he puts behind the ball, the player calculates how much spin to put on the ball. The precise place where the stick stabs the ball determines what spin, if any, the ball will possess. The four basic spins not only guide the cue ball's path, but also the path of any object ball the cue ball taps. Here are some examples:

overspin

Strike the cue ball from above its equator (or waistline), and your stick increases the ball's forward roll. This overspin is perfect for when you want to bump into an object ball and continue moving the cue ball forward, too, rather than having the cue ball stop once it strikes (and transfers energy to) the object ball.

backspin or draw

Strike the cue ball below its equator, and it will reverse direction once it hits the object ball. The backwards spin (or draw) will deaden the cue ball's forward movement when it connects with the object ball, making the cue ball retreat.

sidespin or English

Strike the cue ball on one side or the other, and you'll add sidespin, (also called "English"). When the ball hits a bumper, the angle of its rebound will be greater or lesser, depending on its sidespin. For instance, a clockwise-spinning ball that hits a bumper on the right will have a wider rebound. A counter-clockwise-spinning ball that hits the right bumper will have a narrower rebound.

combination spin

Any strike of the stick on the cue ball can be slightly left or right, slightly high or low. Knowing this, a good player can create a combination spin—movement that's forward/backward and left/right. For instance, striking the cue ball below and to the right of its exact center will give the ball both backspin and sidespin, curving it toward the left.

throw

Although it's not really a spin, it's just as important. As your cue ball hits an object ball, it creates friction, which changes the course of both balls. Aim your cue ball at the right side of an object ball, and you'll send it to the left. Aim to the object ball's left side, and you'll send it to the right.

BALL of FAME

Not-So-Hairy Potter

Who: Dave Pearson of the United Kingdom
Record: He "potted" 15 balls in 26.5 seconds. That means he lined up, shot, and sunk each ball into a pocket. And each ball took him an average of less than 2 seconds!
Any other records? Glad you asked. In 1998, Dave cleared 10 tables in 10 minutes flat. That's 160 balls and an average of 3.5 seconds to get each ball into a pocket.

Odd Balls

● What do Mozart, Thomas Jefferson, Lewis Carroll, W. C. Fields, Mark Twain, Babe Ruth, Frank Sinatra, Henry Ford, Paul Newman, Teddy Roosevelt, General George Custer, Humphrey Bogart, and almost every American president since Eisenhower have in common? They all shared a passion for pool.

Footsie

Who: Paul Sahli of Switzerland, a *balljongleur*. (That's Swiss for ball juggler.)
Record: He juggled a billiard ball for more than 51 minutes, 55 seconds.
So? Just one ball? Like that's hard? He used his *feet*! Paul also holds records for the longest time foot-juggling one tennis ball and for juggling one soccer ball—*while climbing a ladder.*

● Few other sports are so enjoyed by players of all backgrounds, ages, and sexes. Most other sports require more athleticism, devotion, money, coaching—or just plain old youthfulness in order to play even a decent game.

● The average age of a billiard champion is 35.6 years—the oldest of any major sport. Billiards also happens to be considered the safest of any pro sport.

A Tale of Mark Twain

During his time as "an underpaid reporter," Mark Twain played pool for money. Once, the owner of a new billiard's parlor challenged the creator of *Adventures of Huckleberry Finn* and *The Adventures of Tom Sawyer* to a game. The owner had Twain "knock a few balls around" so he could assess the author's skill. Once Twain had pocketed a few balls, the owner announced, "I will be perfectly fair with you. I'll play you left-handed."

Hurt by that remark, Twain later wrote, "I determined to teach him a lesson. He won first shot, ran out, took my half-dollar, and all I got was the opportunity to chalk my cue. 'If you can play like that with your left hand,' I said, 'I'd like to see you play with your right.' 'I can't,' he said. 'I'm left-handed.'"

BALL TALK

Masters of spin and speed, pool players use many shots to move the cue ball toward, around, and even over the other balls. Some shots have some wild names—like the banana shot, garbage shot, jaw shot, nail shot, railroad shot, skyrocket shot, and umbrella shot, but here are a few basic shots:

break shot: *when the cue ball smacks into the racked balls and sends them scurrying across the table. Most billiards games begin with this move.*

bank shot: *when the cue ball hits another ball, and that ball bumps into a rail, bouncing off and into a pocket.*

kick shot: *when the cue ball banks off one or more cushions before it hits another ball or causes it to score.*

feather shot: *a shot in which the cue ball barely touches the object ball, nudging the object ball into the pocket.*

kiss shot: *when the cue ball uses one ball like a bumper to change or correct its course as it moves to pocket or move another ball.*

lemonade stroke: *when you intentionally make a very lousy shot, disguising the fact that you're a good player.*

kill shot: *a shot with backwards spin. When it hits the object ball, the draws "kills" the cue ball's momentum, often preventing it from rolling into a pocket. It's just a term—playing pool isn't usually dangerous.*

Bird's Eye Billiards

Don't expect pool to become the next form of in-flight entertainment, but in 1929, the first sky-high pocket billiards game took place in an airplane above Detroit. The stunt inspired other prominent players to try their hand in a few airborne competitions over the next few years. But a sky-high version of the game just . . . just never took off—maybe because the beverage carts couldn't get around the pool tables.

QUESTION A BALL

Ask the Icosahedron

What ball is used in a game you never win or lose, has a "playing field" as large as your imagination, and requires no other equipment or opposing players?

Stumped? Here's a clue: It's a billiard ball that's too big to drop in the pocket of any billiard table.

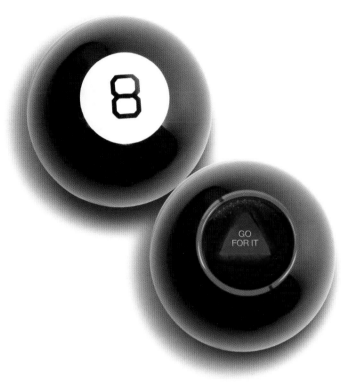

Answer: The Magic 8 Ball! This over-sized billiard ball is flattened on one part of its surface and contains a 20-sided, 3-D object—ah yes, the icosahedron—with answers to any yes-or-no question you dream up.

Invented in 1946, the Magic 8 Ball's good fortune has continued year after year, with Mattel, Inc., creating new answers and designs to this day.

So why did the toy's inventor, Abe Bookman, decide that the black number 8 pool ball was the all-knowing one? Because it's the crucial ball in games of 8-ball? Because 8 is a lucky number in Chinese culture? No one knows for sure—and not even the Magic 8 Ball can give us that answer!

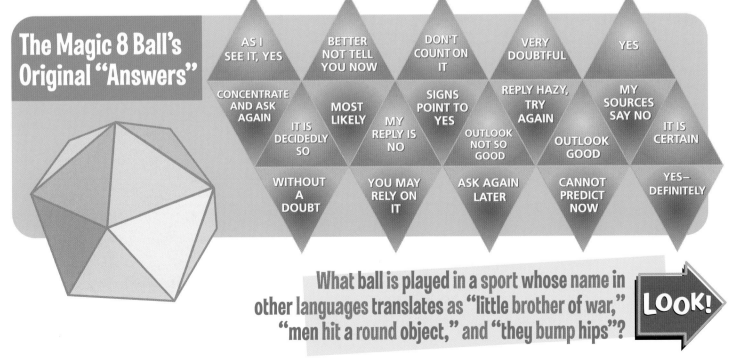

The Magic 8 Ball's Original "Answers"

AS I SEE IT, YES	BETTER NOT TELL YOU NOW	DON'T COUNT ON IT	VERY DOUBTFUL	YES
CONCENTRATE AND ASK AGAIN	MOST LIKELY	SIGNS POINT TO YES	REPLY HAZY, TRY AGAIN	MY SOURCES SAY NO
IT IS DECIDEDLY SO	MY REPLY IS NO	OUTLOOK NOT SO GOOD	OUTLOOK GOOD	IT IS CERTAIN
WITHOUT A DOUBT	YOU MAY RELY ON IT	ASK AGAIN LATER	CANNOT PREDICT NOW	YES— DEFINITELY

What ball is played in a sport whose name in other languages translates as "little brother of war," "men hit a round object," and "they bump hips"? LOOK!

The Lacrosse Ball!

ACTUAL SIZE!

Whack it! Slap it!
Just don't lose your head!

Sports historians often say that America's very first sport is the child of North America's indigenous peoples—a child that the French adopted, the Canadians reared, and now is full-grown. Lacrosse is celebrated in countries around the globe by people who enjoy its mixture of hockey, basketball, and soccer—with a little fencing and way too much amusement-park, bumper-car crashing—at least, in the men's game.

Played by the Six Nations, the indigenous peoples who occupied much of New York, southern Quebec, and Ontario, Canada, the original game was more than a sport. It resolved conflicts, healed the sick, and prepared men for war. In "The Creator's Game," the field had a few more than today's standard twenty players—try a hundred times as many! Two thousand players from the same or different tribes competed on a playing field that wasn't exactly regulation. In fact, players often couldn't see the goal (a rock or pair of trees), because the contest could spread over fifteen miles and last for several days. And since most players were nowhere near the ball, their sticks were less ball-movers than weapons.

During this time period, a game ball could be carved from wood, sewn from deerskin stuffed with hair or stones, molded from hardened clay, or—when a ball was lost or fell apart—cut from atop the neck of a losing team member. Yes, in some of the more than four dozen tribes that played this game, the lowest-ranking tribe member, or the person who lost the ball, would be sacrificed, and his head turned into the new ball.

European pioneers arriving in North America weren't into the head-losing thing. They created a slightly different game in the 1800s and called it "lacrosse," from the French words *le crosse*—because the player's stick reminded them of a cross.

In 1867, Canadian W. George Beers helped to establish the smaller playing field. He, too, figured that future players wouldn't have all week for a single game, let alone miles of traffic-free land on which to play. He also introduced the hard rubber ball, on which today's balls are still modeled.

Modern lacrosse takes more agility, speed, and coordination than strength, size, and brawn. But it's still easy to "lose your head" as you sprint up and down the field, dodge, fake, pass, check, collide—and try to fling that small ball past the goalie to score!

Men's and Women's Lacrosse

Until the 1930s, men and women played the same game of lacrosse, but then the men's game became more aggressive. With more contact came new rules. In turn, women's lacrosse became a faster game without the burden of protective gear.

Both men and women play indoor lacrosse or box lacrosse, which is often held during the summer on an ice rink covered with artificial turf. The biggest difference? Since the playing field is smaller, the game is tougher: The attacking team only has thirty seconds from the time they get possession of the ball to shoot it.

About the riddle on page 65:
Lacrosse is known as Tewaarathon *in the language of the Mohawk people ("little brother of war"),* dehuntshigwa'es *in Onondaga ("men hit a round object"), and* baggattawag *in Ojibwe ("they bump hips").*

THE INSIDE SCOOP

The ball's composition
is solid sponge rubber.

The ball's weight
must be between 5
and 5.25 ounces.

The circumference
must be between
7.75 and 8 inches.

The color
may be white,
yellow, lime green,
or orange,
depending on the
league.

72"

45-49"

Bounce-ablility
When dropped from a
height of 72 inches on
a hardwood floor, the
ball must bounce up
between 45 and 49
inches.

"quote a Ball"

"When you talk about
lacrosse, you talk about the
lifeblood of the Six Nations.
The game is ingrained into
our culture and our system
and our lives."

—Chief Oren Lyons, Iroquois tribal leader,
environmentalist, and human rights advocate

clamping (or trapping): an attempt to seize control of the ball at the face-off by pushing the back of the stick onto the ball.

cradling: rotating the wrists and arms to keep the ball inside the upper part of the stick pocket.

scooping: sliding the pocket toward a ground ball to lift it into the netting.

checking: attempting to jostle the ball from the ball carrier by tapping or jabbing your stick at the ball carrier's stick. There are many kinds of checks, including those that are classified as penalties.

slashing: an "unchecked" jab, striking an opponent's body with the stick anywhere but the gloved hand that's holding the stick.

carrying the pizza (also known as walking the dog): running down the field with the ball carried out in front, arms and stick extended—the opposite of cradling.

Faster Than a Category-Five Hurricane!

If you cross lacrosse with handball, you get a two-person game played on a three-walled court with short, netted sticks that fire and catch the fastest ball flung in any sport! This hard, two-inch-wide ball flies at speeds reaching 168 miles per hour!*

No lie, that's jai alai, or *pelota,* a game with roots near Spain and France. The basic game involves hurling a ball against the front wall with a bare hand, gloved hand, or, in the speediest version, a glove with a wicker basket, or *cesta,* that's bound to the player's arm with tape.

The ball *(see photo at left)* has a hard rubber core, a layer of linen, and then two layers of goatskin, creating a ball that weighs 4.5 ounces—which is about what a bagel, a flamingo chick, a just-born kitten, or a medium banana weighs, in case someone asks you.

* Category Five hurricanes are the most damaging, with wind speeds greater than 155 miles per hour.

Lacrosse Ball Fact

Winners keepers; losers weepers.
The home team supplies all the balls for the game, but the winner gets to keep them.

STicKY BUSiNESS

Like lacrosse and polo, hockey is a game in which opposing teams work up a big sweat by moving a ball into a guarded goal at the opposite end of a field. Egyptologists found drawings on a Nile Valley tomb from 4,000 years ago that depict people hitting a round thing with a long bent thing. (Archaeologists apparently ruled out the possibility that they had developed the first Whac-a-Mole game.) The Greeks, Romans, Ethiopians, and Aztecs each competed in similar games, even though no one had yet invented real hockey jerseys or first-aid kits—essentials in modern hockey.

The field hockey we know took shape in the mid-nineteenth century in England and eventually shipped out to the British colonies, including Pakistan, India, Australia, Canada, and parts of Africa and the Caribbean. Thus, the birth of international competition!

Curiously, at first the game was considered to be too rough for women. But in 1901, Constance Applebee, a British phys. ed. teacher, came to Harvard and saw the "parlor games" college girls were offered as exercise (croquet and lawn tennis).

She staged an impromptu hockey game with borrowed equipment. Faster than a new fashion trend, the game took hold in most women's colleges in the East. Today, field hockey is one of the most popular college sports for women.

And the sport continues to inspire variations. While you've got your field hockey (played on a field) and your ice hockey (played on ice), there are other hockey games played underwater, on skates, on turf-covered indoor rinks—and even played by remote-controlled robots!

THE INSIDE SCOOP

Field hockey balls
are spherical and white, although teams can agree to play with another color.

The composition *is usually a smooth plastic, but other materials are permitted. On wet turf, a dimpled ball is brought into play. The center is hollow; however, some balls do have a cork-and-rubber core.*

The circumference *is between 8.8125 and 9.5 inches.*

The weight *is between 5.25 to 5.5 ounces.*

Two Pair, Four in a Row, or Just One?

Hockey on Wheels

Roller hockey is played on quad skates that have paired wheels, one set in front and one set in back. James Plympton invented these skates in 1863 for a game called "rink hockey," originally adapted from polo. In fact, the game was first called "roller polo."

In America, three types of roller hockey are played today: hardball hockey uses a hard rubber ball; North American hockey uses a softer (and safer) ball; and puck hockey uses a light-weight puck, similar in shape but much lighter than an ice-hockey puck. All three fast-paced games feel more like soccer or basketball, with dazzling footwork, hairpin turns, and screeching halts, thanks to the greater control and maneuverability of the quad-wheel placement.

Inline hockey, played on skates with four wheels lined up like an ice skate's blade, doesn't permit the quick turns or abrupt stops, so these games are speedy but with more sprinting back and forth across the field. (By the way, did you know that the very first skates, made in 1820, were inline skates?)

Inline hockey teams sometimes use a ball, but typically it's the puck they're after.

Want to play one-wheel hockey? Hop on a unicycle! Instead of skates, players mount a unicycle and try to score goals with a "dead" tennis ball. It's a kinder, gentler hockey—no checking allowed—since it's hard enough just keeping your balance while swinging a stick.

THE INSIDE SCOOP

Roller hockey hardballs
usually have a core of cork and rubber.

The circumference *must be 9 inches.*

The weight *is 5.5 ounces.*

The ball's color *must contrast with the playing surface, either black or orange.*

Extreme ODD Balls

When it comes to balls, there must be some unwritten rule that says, "If it's bigger, it's better." For instance, some sports museums have a ball that spans their entranceways or fills their lobbies. Water towers around the country are shaped or painted to champion their communities' favorite sport's balls. There's certainly another unwritten rule that reads, "The bigger the ball, the harder it is to make," because some folks have spent years—decades!—creating monster balls from miniature parts and mind-boggling efforts. Here are some oversized examples to inspire you.

Oh, Quit Your Twining!

The world's biggest ball of twine is 8 feet tall, measures 40 feet around, and weighs 9 tons (that's 17,980 pounds—about 100 lacrosse players rolled into one.) Unraveled, the ball's 7,827,737 feet of sisal (a fiber used to make rope and twine) could stretch from Manhattan, New York, to Key West, Florida (1,444 miles). Started in 1953 by Frank Stoeber, the ball continues to expand during an annual "twine-a-thon" in Cawker City, Kansas.

You Can't Shoot This PAINT BALL

Starting with a regulation baseball, Mike and Glenda Carmichael of Alexandria, Indiana, have brushed a rainbow of colors onto the ball for more than 30 years—so far, it's had more than 20,100 coats of paint! Weighing over a ton, with a "waist" of 133 inches, it's the world's largest paint ball. (BTW: If you were to slug this ball with a bat of the same proportional weight, you'd be swinging a 12,800-pound bat. Now that would take a real power hitter!)

My Pop's Bigger Than Your Pop

Picture a baseball-size popcorn ball. If you're the average American, that's about 1/150 of the 54 quarts of popcorn you'll eat this year. Now imagine a popcorn ball that's 50,000 times bigger—the sort of snack that King Kong might enjoy at the movies. Weighing in a 3,423 pounds—the ball, not the gorilla—and standing 8 feet tall, this record-breaking popcorn ball is the concoction of The Popcorn Factory folks, who pop close to a million pounds of popcorn every year over in Illinois. (Fun Food Fact: The shelf life of popcorn is one of the longest of any food. One-thousand-year-old kernels will still pop. One-thousand-year-old melted butter, on the other hand, is gross.)

Whoosh . . .

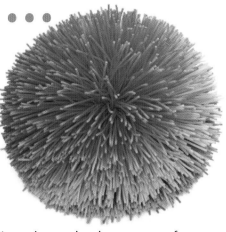

Ever play with "an amusement device which has a substantially spherical configuration...formed from a large plurality of floppy, elastomeric filaments that radiate in a dense, bushy manner from a central core region"? Bet you have! It's a Koosh® Ball. That quote from inventor Scott Stillinger's patent, describes the springy, stringy ball of rubber bands that even young kids can catch. Here's why: Most balls don't absorb energy when caught—they bounce away! Plus, most little kids catch with their eyes closed, which sort of increases the number of dropped balls. Stillinger's cushy, smooshy, 5,000-rubber-strand ball (held together with a hidden ring), collapses, absorbs energy, and even sighs its own name when caught: *Koosh!*

More Bounce to the Ounce

The largest rubber-band ball created by one person stands 5 feet tall and weighs 3,120 pounds. John Bain's record-breaking ball (*see photo at right*) is composed of 850,000 rubber bands and cost nearly $25,000 to create. He says, "I spent about two hours a day in my garage for over five years, wrapping bands, dodging broken bands . . . trying to keep the ball round. It's real exercise. I've also made the world's largest bicycle-inner-tube ball and the world's only rubber-band couch and coffee table."

Steve Milton and his son created an even bigger ball. Breaking with tradition, they linked 175,000 rubber bands into chains that encircle the ball. Their creation weighs 4,595 pounds and has a 19-foot circumference.

An earlier record holder from the United Kingdom, Tony Evans, created a ball with 6 million rubber bands! During an episode of *Ripley's Believe It or Not*, his 2,600-pound ball was released from a helicopter one mile above the Arizona Desert. How high do you think it bounced? Hitting the ground at 400 mph, it created a 9-foot-deep crater, a big dust cloud . . . and no bounce.

Riddle: What Is **Superboy's** Favorite Toy?

Here are a few hints: It has 92 percent bounce-ability—that's three times a tennis ball's rebound power. It can leap over a three-story building. It is made of Zectron® (no, not Kryptonite), which some folks say is a cross between an East Indian rubber plant and an Outer Mongolian plum tree. Every day, about 170,000 of them are made, and when it first came on the scene in 1965 it was so instantly popular that 7 million balls sold in the first six months. Got the answer?

It's the Superball!

Wham-O's legendary bouncer is composed of polybutadene, a synthetic rubber with added sulfur, zinc oxide, antioxidants, and colorants. The mixture is molded for 20 minutes at 320°F at a pressure of 1,000 pounds per square inch. No wonder it bounces like a . . . well, super ball!

Oh, and have you heard of the Super Bowl, that championship game played with that sad excuse for a sphere, the football? Guess what it was named after. Yep.

The **Silliest** Ball of All

It sinks if it's round, floats if it's flat, stretches if it's pulled, breaks if it's jerked, hatches from an egg, and is known to have orbited the Earth. Wait a second! It's from outer space? Not exactly, but astronauts aboard the Apollo VIII spacecraft used this ball to hold their tools in place.

During World War II, rubber was rationed, and General Electric chemists who were experimenting with boric acid and silicone oil in search of a substitute accidentally created a liquid (yes, this ball is a liquid, not a solid!) with bodacious bouncing ability and enormous elasticity. It could also withstand extreme heat or cold, and coincidentally, transfer ink from comic books onto its surface. Every day, Binney & Smith, Inc., in Pennsylvania continues to "hatch" 20,000 eggs—that's 600 pounds—of Silly Putty balls.

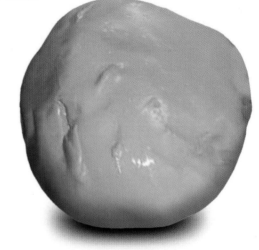

Big PINK

The biggest naturally occurring balls in the world are abalone pearls. (No, your giant pink scoop of peppermint ice cream is not natural.) So far, the record for the largest pearl is 2.76" by 1.97" by 1.1" and can be found in Salt Point State Park, California. In terms of carats (that's how jewels are weighed), the pearl tipped the scales at 469.13 carats (just over 3.33 ounces). Valued at $4.7 million back in 1991, the pearl has been given the name "Big Pink," although it doesn't really answer to that.

IncrediBALL EdiBalls!

Matzo Ball Madness

In less than five and a half minutes, Eric "Badlands" Booker ate twenty-one baseball-sized matzo balls at Ben's Delicatessen's annual competition. Eric's other first-place records include scarfing down pumpkin pies, doughnuts, and burritos. And—talking about ediBALLS— Eric can chomp up more than half a pound of raw Maui onions in sixty seconds and nine and a half pounds of peas in twelve minutes.

Rice Race

Takeru Kobayashi, rated #1 by the International Federation of Competitive Eating, has eaten more bratwursts, cow brains, hamburgers, and hot dogs in less time than anyone else. And his ediBALL record is twenty pounds of rice balls in thirty minutes. That's as much as a hefty Thanksgiving turkey. Talk about being stuffed!

On Top of Spaghetti

Hey, hold the spaghetti! Sonya Thomas devoured ten pounds, four and a half ounces of meatballs in twelve minutes. She holds twenty-one other eating records, ranging from baked beans to fruitcake.

Got Room for Mushroom?

What ball is of no use on any playing field; is found underground; enjoyed by people, dogs, and pigs; and costs four times as much as a solid gold ball of the same size? It's a white truffle—and we're talking fungus, not chocolate! This firm, round mushroom is mostly found in Italy and France. A few years ago, three restaurants chipped in to buy a rare, enormous one-pound truffle for $35,000.

FOR FURTHER READING

SOME INTERESTING BOOKS AND WEB SITES TO BOUNCE AROUND

Sports and Balls in General

Fortin, Francis, editor. *Sports: The Complete Visual Reference*. Ontario: Firefly Books, reprint edition, 2003. Another great reference guide that's also incredibly fun to flip through. This one features more than 200 sports with smart graphics and easy-to-understand text.

Galahad Books, publisher of the How to Talk series. The series includes *How to Talk Baseball* (by Mike Whiteford, and Dick Schaap) and *How to Talk Bowling* (by Dawson Taylor). Each book contains definitions of "ball talk" with lively illustrations by Taylor Jones.

Web Sites

www.sportsknowhow.com
A site that shares the history, rules, and basic game play of many sports, including baseball, bocce, hockey, lacrosse, pickleball, and softball.

www.americanhistory.si.edu/sports/
The Smithsonian Institution's traveling exhibit, "Breaking Records, Breaking Barriers," can also be seen online. It features profiles on inventors, Olympians, and heroic athletes—as well as highlighting sports memorabilia from the earliest skates to collectible baseballs. Check out the great list of books selected just for kids about sports figures.

www.mastersgames.com/rules/rules.htm
Specializing in table, lawn, and outdoor games, including basic information and rules about billiards, bowling, bocce, and croquet.

Baseball

Cook, Sally and James Charlton, illustrated by Ross MacDonald. *Hey, Batta Batta, Swing! The Wild Old Days of Baseball*. New York: Simon & Schuster, 2007. A narrative portrait of baseball's early days, painted with surprising facts, lots of "ball talk," and sports trivia.

Gutman, Dan, with an introduction by Tim McCarver, *The Way Baseball Works*. New York: Simon & Schuster, 1996. Produced with the National Baseball Hall of Fame, this book is a home run of information on the game's evolution, mechanics, and strategies.

Wills, Brett, *Baseball Archeology: Artifacts from the Great American Pastime*. San Francisco: Chronicle Books, 1993. Beautiful photographs of vintage equipment, tracing the history of the game in America.

Wong Stephen, Smithsonian *Baseball: Inside the World's Finest Private Collections*. New York: HarperCollins, 2005. A huge photographic album of sports memorabilia.

www.exploratorium.edu/baseball/index.html
The "exhibits" at this site include: how balls bounce, how to throw curve balls, famous female ball players, Japanese baseball, and cool animations of slugging and pitching.

www.baseballhalloffame.org
The online home of the Baseball Hall of Fame has virtual exhibits and "Electronic Field Trips," including feature-length videos and podcasts on topics that include "Slide into History," "Science of the Sandlot," and "Dirt on Their Skirts" (women in baseball).

Softball

www.fastpitchsoftball.com
This site has everything: softball jokes and cheers from around the country, team drills, softball history, and even flash-animation batting games.

www.whitehouse.gov/tball
Find out about the annual T-ball games on the White House lawn and read the "Ask the White House" Q&A with major guest players, such as Nolan Ryan and Cal Ripken, Jr. There's also a link (www.whitehouse.gov/baseball/) that takes you to a photo history of the Presidents' love of most all-American sport.

www.whiffleball.org
Home of the World Whiffleball Championship, this site has a hilarious history of "The Strange, but True, History of Whiffleball on Planet Earth," a hall of fame, and a news archive all about the game.

Bowling

Bosker, Gideon and Bianca Lencek-Bosker. Bowled Over: Roll Down Memory Lane. San Francisco: Chronicle Books, 2002. Here are 128 pages of vintage images and fascinating lore from the heyday of American bowling culture.

Nace, Don, illustrated with photographs by Bruce Curtis. Bowling for Beginners: Simple Steps to Strikes & Spares. New York: Sterling, 2001. A manual that covers pretty much everything—scoring, etiquette, throwing tips, gear—for a new bowler.

www.bowl.com/youth/
The United States Bowling Congress has a Web site for young bowlers with a variety of information about leagues, current records, and tips—as well as online games, computer wallpaper, and links.

Bocce

Collins, Bud. *Total Tennis: The Ultimate Tennis Encyclopedia.* Toronto: Sport Classic Books, 2003. A giant volume, gathering most everything about the sport.

www.bocce.com
The United States Bocce Federation's site has descriptions, diagrams, and photographs that show all the basic plays and shots in the different forms of the game.

www.petanque.org
A site of "boules around the world," features vintage artwork and concise histories of many types of throwing games.

www.mastersgames.com/rules/petanque-rules.htm
www.mastersgames.com/rules/bowls-rules.htm
Masters Traditional Games is an Internet store from the United Kingdom that sells every sort of game equipment—all interesting to see!—but they also offer a user-friendly guide to bocce, boule, bowls, petanque, as well as croquet and billiard games.

Croquet

Boga, Steve. Croquet (Backyard Games). Mechanicsburg, PA: Stackpole, 1995. All the basics of the game, from setting up the wickets to winning strategies.

www.croquetamerica.com/new/
The United States Croquet Association presents a comprehensive listing of all the games with their many variations and rules and features short video clips and articles on the game's history.

www.croquet.org.uk/
The United Kingdom Croquet Association's site has videos of croquet shots, a summary of the basic games, and lots of help with techniques and strategies.

Shot put

Carr, Gerald A. Fundamentals of Track and Field. Champagne, IL: Human Kinetics. Second edition, 1999. A technical book for athletes and coaches that outlines the various running, jumping, and throwing events.

www.highlandgames.net/
A site about Scottish Heavy Athletics that includes videos and frame-by-frame "stop action" shots of athletes throwing the stones, hammer, caber, and sheaf.

www.throwfarther.org/vidoes/index.html
Short video clips of shot putters. (Also clips of hammer- and discus-throwers.)

Billiards

Bryne, Robert. Bryne's New Standard Book of Pool and Billiards. New York: Harvest/Harcourt, 1998. This updated authority, at 432 pages, is mainly grown-up reading, but it's packed with illustrations and lively entries on every aspect of these table games. You can read about the fundamentals or just pick a few of the hundreds of strategies and trick shots he explains.

www.bca-pool.com
The Billiard Congress of America Web site has clear rules for a variety of pocket pool games, a Hall of Fame, information about junior leagues, and standards for all billiard equipment and competitions.

www.poolplayers.com/drcue/index.html
The American Poolplayers Association has a great section of instructional video clips that includes trick shots and basic techniques with Tom "Dr. Cue" Rossman.

Lacrosse and Hockey

www.nll.com/laxoverview.php
The National Lacrosse League's Webs site hosts "LAX 101"—anything you'd want to know about the elements of lacrosse plays, the game's history, and "Terms of the Turf."

www.lacrosse.org
The Web site of U.S. Lacrosse has men's, women's, and youth lacrosse team information and standings, official rules for each division, as well as a virtual tour of their Lacrosse Museum and Hall of Fame: www.lacrosse.org/museum/index.phtml#

www.usfieldhockey.com
A member of the U.S. Olympic teams, the USA Field Hockey's site describes the sport's rules, traditions, equipment, and history, plus news about the teams and upcoming games.

Oddballs

www.worldslargestthings.com/ worldslargestthings.htm
The World's Largest Things site gathers the largest known example of just about everything: cups, walleyes, doughnuts, yo-yos—and plenty of ball-shaped things, too. Some are featured as postcards, while other feature links to their respective Web sites.

www.thelongestlistofthelongeststuffatthe- longestdomainnameatlonglast.com/
That pretty must says it all. Search for articles and records on the "longest" sushi roll, stone skip, hockey game, or group hug. Hundreds of entries and links to follow.

www.ifoce.com/contests.php
The International Federation of Competitive Eating is the record-holding organization for eating contests around the world.

INDEX

For *Balls!* (in red) and *Balls! Round 2* (in blue)